Crewe Remembered

By

Allan C Baker

IRWELL PRESS Ltd.

ISBN 1-903266-52-1

Dedication

Stephen Allan Baker

No son could have wanted a finer father, one who helped and mentored me so much. My memories of happy times together are legion.

First published in the United Kingdom in 2005
by Irwell Press Limited, 59A, High Street, Clophill,
Bedfordshire MK45 4BE
Printed by Interprint, Malta

Contents

Page 5	**Foreword**	
Page 9	**Introduction**	
Page 15	**Chapter One**	A Railwayman at Last – Life at Crewe North
Page 33	**Interval 1:**	Crewe Generalities
Page 47	**Chapter Two**	Examination and Repair Depot – 'Crewe Diesel Depot'
Page 61	**Chapter Three**	Points and Signals
Page 77	**Interval 2:**	Crewe Surroundings
Page 83	**Chapter Four**	The Perth Job

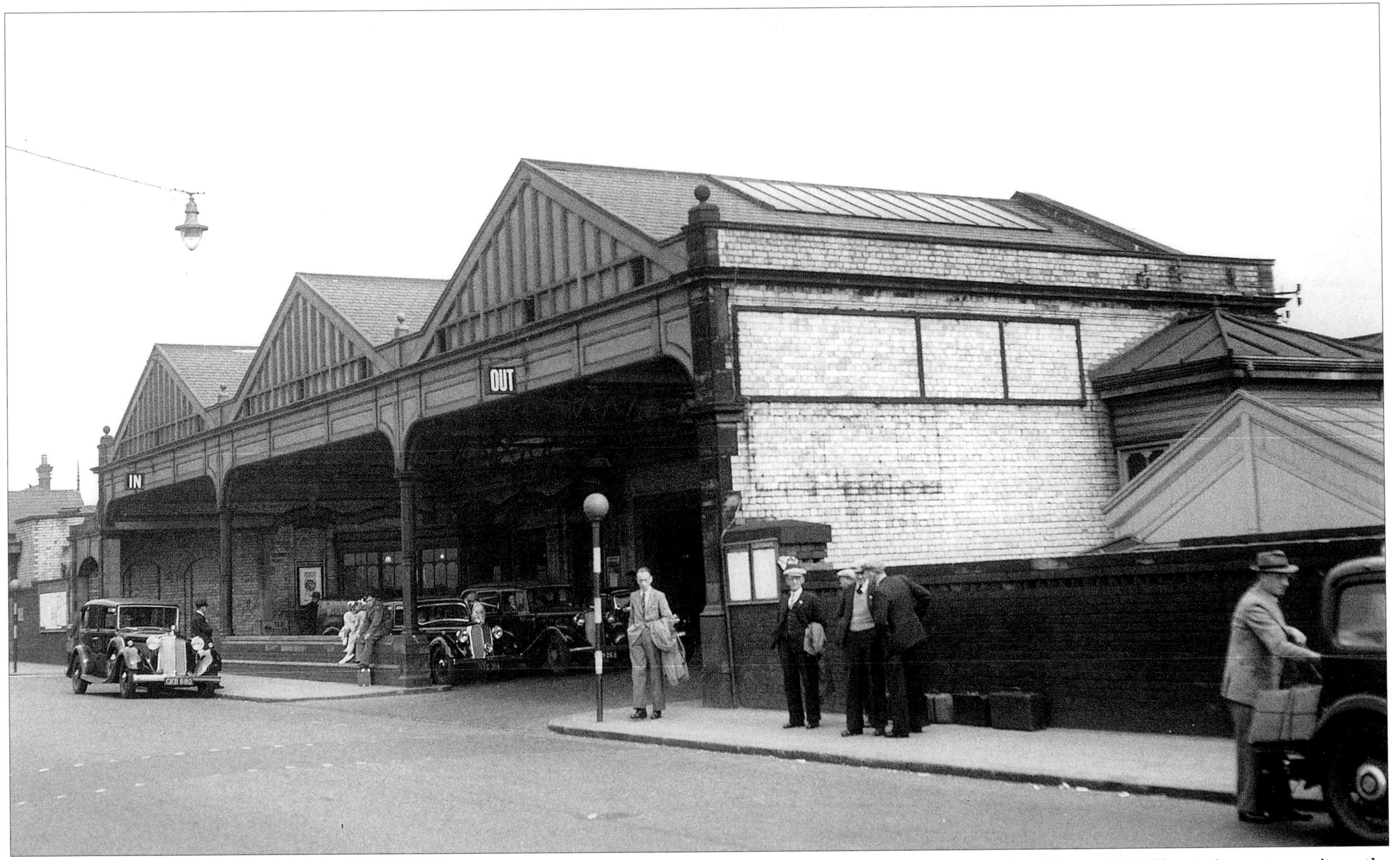

Crewe Station is bisected by the main thoroughfare between the old market towns of Sandbach and Nantwich, the Nantwich Road, later A534. The station entrance is on the bridge taking the road over the railway and has had to be successively rebuilt as the station was enlarged and road traffic increased. Indeed, the most recent bridge rebuilding was but a few years ago. This is the station entrance looking south on 1 July 1950, a simple affair belying the importance of the station below but then Crewe is more famous as a place to change trains, rather than starting or finishing journeys, and this is still the case. For many years the traditional Crewe Works holidays were the first two weeks in July, and doubtless the gents in suits and with cases would be railwaymen. (MN Bland, Transport Treasury)

Foreword

Unashamedly I declare this book as very much an Allan Baker book about Crewe, rather than a Crewe book by Allan Baker. And yes I know, I said something on similar lines in the Preface to *Crewe Sheds* (Ian Allan, 1988) which consisted of my words and Gavin Morrison's efforts with the photography. For here is a very personal collection or essays on various aspects of Crewe and its locomotives. My choice has largely centred on personal memories and activities but the discovery of a super collection of studies taken during the 1940 re-signalling works meant I could not resist a chapter describing something of this. I am sure readers, especially model makers, will welcome them. Of course I am no signalling expert, but I do hope readers will feel I have done them justice, in both the relevant chapter and the individual captions.

I have written here at length on my early life as a railwayman at Crewe North shed, despite having done so too in *Crewe Sheds* but I do not think I have repeated much. Despite the fact that I spent but two and a half years there, this period comes back to me now as clear as any in my 40-plus years in the industry. I had always wanted to be a railwayman, and locomotives were my first love, and are still very high in my scheme of things. So to be placed among them, in such an intimate way and at the tender age of but 15 years and a month, satisfied my wildest dreams, and I enjoyed every minute of it. I took notes – had done from early schoolboy days – and continue to do so today! I also made it my business to talk to my colleagues, both fitting staff and footplate men, such that I made many friends some of whom I remain in contact with today. At the expense of repeating words from *Crewe Sheds*, I am extremely proud to have spent the first few years of my apprenticeship at what to me was the premier locomotive shed of the Premier Line, the London & North Western Railway. It was great to work alongside men who had started their careers on the old North Western and to hear tales of times past, of those fiery black monsters that made that railway such an icon among enthusiasts of the day. It continues to enjoy a strong following these 80 odd years after it ceased to exist!

I have also chosen to write about what is now Crewe Diesel Depot, both as it has a very interesting history and because I spent some six years of my life working there, as an apprentice, fitter, inspector and later a foreman. Last but by no means least, I have chosen to write about a trip I made on a Duchess Pacific to Perth and back, because so little has been written about the work of these magnificent locomotives going about their nightly wanderings. For they did just as much work at night as they did in daylight, and in train spotting days I used to wonder where they all were. If one stood at the line side as I did south of Crewe on the West Coast Main Line – a few miles from my native Stoke-on-Trent – you'd be lucky to see more than seven or eight in as many hours. They would appear on the up and down Royal Scot, Mid-Day Scot and, after its introduction, The Caledonian. There would also be two or three Princess Royals on the Liverpools – just where *were* all the others I used to ponder? Even a day spent at Crewe on the platforms would not produce many more and the North Shed was impenetrable to spotters!

But eventually I found out that they worked the heavy night trains between Crewe, Glasgow and Perth and this explained why the Crewe North allocation, which one might have expected to easily 'cop' at Crewe, were among the most elusive on trains going south. I was very

Looking north along No.4 Platform on 4 October 1956, with a London to Blackpool train in. There is a wealth of detail to be absorbed here, but of particular note is the Wymans bookstall – there is still a bookstall in this exact position today. The mobile refreshment trolley and the various signs are still pure LNWR! What a lot of people travelling, and it's October remember, well outside the holiday season.

Duchess Pacific 46230 DUCHESS OF BUCCLEUCH, a long-time Polmadie resident; apart from a year or so when new, it was there all its life. She is backing on to a train at the north end of Platform 2. The train would almost certainly be one from London to Glasgow and would have come down with either a Camden or Crewe North engine. Notice the well-coaled tender, slight steam leakage from the coal pusher and the 'feather' from the safety valves. The fireman would have a good fire ready for the trip, and by judicious use of the injectors just keep the engine from blowing off; note too, the express headlamps already in position – contrary to regulations! The Duchess would have been waiting on the adjacent road for this train, together with the van that it is about to attach. A timeless view from the early to mid-1950s, unless some reader knows when the platform awning repairs were undertaken, which would date it more accurately. (Alan Robinson – Ashley Archive)

young at the time I made my trip, and the diesels had already started to penetrate the workings, but to my everlasting satisfaction I did make the journey once with a 'Big 'Un', as Crewe men always called these engines. I first wrote the chapter over 25 years ago at the request of the late lamented Derek Cross, for a book he was planning on the Stanier Pacifics. His untimely death meant the book never appeared and the draft has remained in my files gathering dust every since. I did consider using it in *Crewe Sheds* but for reasons I cannot now even recall I never did. Anyway here it is, and I do hope it helps to illuminate an aspect of the work of these locomotives – of which so little has ever appeared in print.

Having spent the first twelve years of my working life at Crewe, I have a tremendous affection for the place and as my professional life takes me there occasionally I am able to indulge that affection. However, I have watched the railway influence there diminish, particularly over the last few years as large parts of the Works have been demolished and roadways and supermarkets built in its place. Whilst nostalgia comes into play when I see all this, it is nevertheless gratifying to see Bombardier Transportation Limited (the present owners of the Works) spending money to develop the place, with great enthusiasm. I am a great supporter of the Crewe Dinner, held annually in London and going back to the days of F.W. Webb. This event was a part of the annual weekend in London by the Crewe Premium Apprentices and was presided over by the Locomotive Chief of the day. It continues under slightly different membership rules, and is now also supported by industry players as a hospitality occasion; nevertheless, it still forms a gathering of 'Crewe Men' past and present, and whilst I cannot claim to be one in either the true definition of a Premium Apprentice, or today's equivalent, I can claim to be Crewe trained, albeit in the old Motive Power Department and at the famous North Shed! It is for me one of the highlights of the railway year.

It remains for me to thank those who have helped my in my efforts, and in doing so I would single out for special mention Phil Pepper. Phil is about my age and would have started at Crewe North around the same time, albeit in his case on the footplate. He has during his time fired the Pacifics and recently completed his career as a Driver with Wales & West, working trains to and from Cardiff. Phil, who still lives near Crewe, has been a tremendous help to me over the years, maintaining as he does connections with many old colleagues. Charlie Oxley was the first Shed Master at Crewe Diesel and today, as a retired Deputy Chief Mechanical Engineer of the New Zealand Government Railway, is a regular correspondent. Peter Rowledge, himself the author of many books about LMS locomotives, was at one time in charge of Crewe Diesel, and is another of my 'Crewe correspondents'. I made mention in the book *Crewe Sheds* of all those fine fellows I worked with, a great many of whom are no longer with us, and I singled out Geoff Oliver as an outstanding example. I can do no better therefore, than to thank Geoff once again not only for all the help and inspiration he gave me as an apprentice and young fitter, but also more recently for reminiscing over old times.

On the photography front, then of course I thank all those who have allowed their work to be used. Of special mention is Michael Mensing who has once again dug out all his excellent material for me to choose from, and my old fiend and co-author

Gavin Morrison. For many years now Gavin and I have had a hankering to write a book on the LMS Pacifics and with semi-retirement looming for me we might do just that! I would also like to mention the late George Wheeler of Southampton. George was a prolific photographer with a great liking for big engines, and in almost all the Ian Allan ABCs from the mid-1950s to the end of steam, one or more of his locomotive portraits will be found. George made it his business to get to know the management at a number of sheds, including Crewe North, and some of his work I have used in this book. Knowing the limitations of his equipment he stuck in the main to static subjects, and some wonderful work resulted. I first came across George when I was at Finsbury Park diesel depot in the early 1970s, because he had got to know the Kings Cross men at Top Shed and continued the relationship at Finsbury Park with the Deltics. And later, when I was Depot Engineer at Eastleigh we became firm friends – what a great pity he died so early. John Bucknall, an old friend from Stafford, has also rallied to my cause, for he is another lover of big engines, along with Jim Hardy, one of John's friends. Last but by no means least, Brian Stephenson has come to my help with one of the late W.J.V. Anderson's magnificent Duchess shots; although this will be an old friend I am sure, to anybody interested in these engines, it is an absolute must in any book that talks about these engines working to Perth. I am so pleased to be able to use it here, for in my mind it so epitomises what these engines were all about. Any photographs not individually credited are either of my taking, from my collection, or from the collection of the publishers.

In publishers Chris Hawkins and George Reeve an author could not ask for more and I have largely been left to my own devices with this book. Their enthusiasm and support however, is outstanding, and the relationships built up by them with authors and contributors are in my experience second to none. I salute them and their company and I hope it goes on from strength to strength for a very long time, for I feel they have, over a relatively small number of years, put railway publishing onto a completely different, and very welcome plane.

Almost last but by no means least, my heartfelt appreciation must go the late Geoff Sands for without him my career, whilst I am sure it would have involved railways, would have taken on a different tack. What a great shame Geoff died so early in life, having only recently left the railway as main line steam disappeared. His first love was the steam locomotive and as Engineer in Chief at the Bressingham Steam Museum, working for Alan Bloom, he was in his element. With the use of steam on the main lines again in recent times, Geoff would have been in great demand, but I am glad I managed to visit him at Bressingham while he was still in harness there.

Of course my wife Angela and my Son Kevin, continue to allow me to indulge in my hobby, spending hours 'salted' away in my study and with all the paraphernalia that goes with such a pastime. As a lifelong railwayman they have had to put up with a lot; long and unsociable hours and six house moves in just double that number of years. I owe a lot to them for their understanding and support. And finely, I pay tribute to my parents for their support over the years, particularly the early ones of my career. And a special word for my late father for he was a truly wonderful Dad, who never tired in his support and sacrifice for my sister and I, and who was my very best friend. I miss him greatly for he followed my career so closely, and although in living so far apart we saw little of each other latterly, we were closer than can ever be imagined. Therefore, I have dedicated this book to Dad; it is not the first time I have done so, and I doubt it will not be the last!

Allan C Baker,
Highfield House,
High Halden,
Kent. TN26 3LD

March 2005

The down Shamrock, Euston to Liverpool, awaiting the right away signal at Crewe No.1 Platform on 12 August 1961 (on Saturdays it did not stop at Crewe). At this date on weekdays it left Euston at 4.30pm, was due out of Crewe at 8.2pm, and into Liverpool Lime Street at 9pm. The locomotive on this occasion is Type 4 diesel D306, allocated to Edge Hill at the time and obviously quite new. Notice that the nose end ladder has now been removed, but still no yellow warning panel. On the right can be seen the end of the Crewe North breakdown train, stabled in Welsh's Siding with a very antiquated ex-LNWR vehicle at the end. The concrete bridge was the walkway to the North shed but it was hardly ever used and most staff, including myself, got to the shed by crossing the lines! (Michael Mensing)

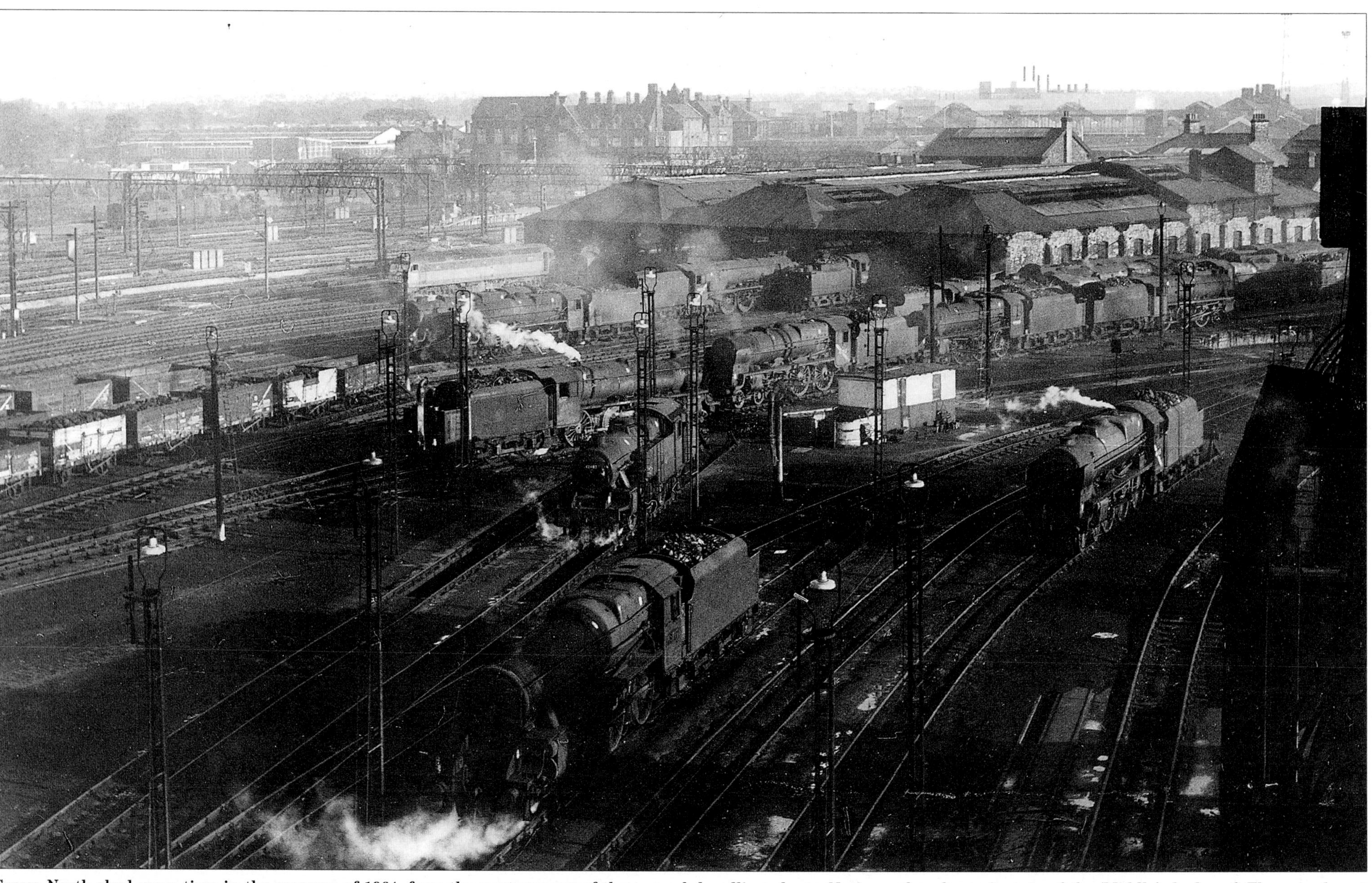

Crewe North shed some time in the summer of 1964, from the westernmost of the two ash handling plants. Notice rather decrepit state of the 'Middle' shed roof. The raised part indicates the wheel drop and shear legs. I would say that this was a Sunday, judging by the number of locomotives present; to the extreme right are two WR engines including a Manor. The rebuilt Patriot in the centre is 45512 BUNSEN, a Carlisle engine at the time. Diesels occupy the far roads and the diagonal yellow stripes on the cabs of the bigger engines confirm this to be the summer of 1964. The station lies beyond. (Jim Hardy)

INTRODUCTION

Crewe. What thoughts this name conjures up in the enthusiast mind: *'Oh Mr Porter what can I do, I wanted to go to Birmingham and they took me on to Crewe'.* My associations with this railway Mecca go back well into childhood days. We lived in Newcastle-under-Lyme and Dad used to take me there on Saturday mornings, by train of course, from our local station at Etruria, for a morning's 'train spotting'. He bought me my first Ian Allan ABC at the bookstall on the old Platform 5, the 1955-56 Winter Edition for the London Midland Region, and I have it still.

Obviously there are many memories of these occasions and a couple will have to suffice. Firstly, Duchess Pacific 46229 DUCHESS OF HAMILTON, just out of works and in immaculate condition arriving at Platform 6 on a running-in turn from Chester, when the Driver invited us on to the footplate – she was still in green and looked a picture. We spent several minutes, were shown the fire, sat in the driver's seat, handled the regulator and all the other things kindly engine drivers show young boys – I would have been about nine at the time. Secondly, being invited into the cab of Patriot 45511 ISLE OF MAN, at the north end of Platform 5 during a station stop while working a northbound express, again a kindly driver of advancing years put me in his seat and Dad took a photograph.

Since those days I have had a soft spot for Stanier's Pacifics, especially in green, and Baby Scots as I came to call them. Later when I became a little more independent I used to take the train to Crewe myself on Saturdays and during school holidays, and I started to take notes – I still have all my notebooks too!

There was of course, much to see at Crewe in those days and even on Saturday mornings a string of engines would be hauled off the Works about 12 o'clock, all freshly overhauled, or new, en route to the South Shed before entering service. The Works was still building Standard 9F 2-10-0s at the time, and I saw several in this way. Highlights were the Up and Down Royal Scot and Mid-Day Scot, the former with its Camden-based Pacific working through to Carlisle, and the latter always changing engines at Crewe with Crewe North engines on both north and south legs. During some summers I recall Polmadie Pacifics arriving, but I never remember them going through to London except on special workings. I had usually left for home by the time the Up Mid-Day was due, but I remember when the Caledonian was introduced *without* a stop at Crewe, an unheard of event in those days. How dare they we all thought!

The main places for the 'spotters' were the north end of Nos.3-4 platforms and the bridge that used to span the tracks at that end of the station, and until we were moved on by some 'official' or other, the bridge that crossed from the north end of No.1 platform to the North Shed. From this vantage point we could not only keep an eye on all the moves around the station, but also the engines on goods and mineral trains using the Independent Lines. These passed through a tunnel under the North Junction, which we knew as the 'Muck Hole'. This was also a good point to attempt to 'bunk' the North Shed (i.e., get in and look around without permission – always refused) which I only tried once, unsuccessfully! Others occasionally made it, but never seemed to penetrate its depths very far before being herded out again. Great fun!

One of the highlights of a visit, and usually before I left for home at a little after 5 o'clock, was the arrival of the through train from Aberystwyth behind an immaculate Western Region Manor 4-6-0. With shining brass and copper work, it used to really brighten up the south end of the station. The distinctive noise of a Western Region engine with the vacuum pump driven from the cross head and the sharp exhaust always fascinated me, even though this particular working was confined to a handful of particular engines. I never tired of this splendid sight and sound. The engine almost always seemed to be either 7800 TORQUAY MANOR; 7801 ANTHONY MANOR; 7802 BRADLEY MANOR or 7803 BARCOTE MANOR. These four were based on the Cambrian section for many a year, and there were others too.

Having said this of course I was, and indeed still am, a dedicated London & North Western enthusiast and as would be expected of a native of the Potteries, the North Staffordshire Railway too. One of, if not the first 'proper' railway book I bought was Nock's *London & North Western Railway* when it was first published in 1960. By 'proper' I mean as opposed to ABCs, Ian Allan *Loco Spotters* and *Trains Annuals*, and other

The author in the cab of Patriot 45511 ISLE OF MAN, at the north end of platform 4 at Crewe on one of his Saturday morning visits with his father. The date is March 1957, and I would have been nine years old at the time. A typical kindly driver looks on; notice his two jackets, it was March after all. Notice, in the cab, the piece of waste on top of the right-hand injector feed clack. These engines never had a Stanier type top feed arrangement. This was a Camden engine at the time, probably working a Blackpool or Heysham train. I do not know if this occasion prompted it, but these were always among my favourite locomotives, perhaps it was their connection with the old LNWR. What a shame one was not saved. (The late SA Baker)

Although not a particularly good photograph, it is one taken by my father on one of our Saturday morning visits to Crewe. This is brand new Standard 9F 2-10-0 92124, in a string of repaired engines being hauled from the Works to the South shed prior to going into traffic – its first allocation was Wellingborough. It is recorded as entering service on 2 March 1957, so the picture would have been taken about that time. The North shed buildings are behind. On another occasion I recall Pacific 46247 CITY OF LIVERPOOL in similar circumstances, the first one we had seen in the then new maroon livery. (The late SA Baker)

books directed more at youngsters – not that I decry these in any way. Dad took *The Railway Magazine* and had a run back to the early 1920s, and I started to take *Railway World* in 1960 when Ian Allan took it over. My cousin Roy took *Trains Illustrated* and he used to pass these on to me – and I still have them, now nicely bound!

I was fascinated by those fiery looking immaculate LNW black engines I saw in Dad's old 'Railway Mags', all with that family likeness, sharp angles to their running plates and cabs, and a general boxy look – and I so much liked the 'Super D's' of which there were plenty about, both in and around Crewe as well as my native Stoke-on-Trent. Their distinctive exhaust when working hard of two long, one short and a wheeze, fascinated me. Although out of print by this time I found a copy of Nock's *Premier Line* in the local Library, and read over and over again this history of the North Western engines along with his *Railway Race to the North* – what splendid reading. Often now, in the late evening at weekends when the family have retired to bed, I relax with my pint, and re-read these super volumes – Nock at his very best!

To return to those trips to Crewe and to give but one example of what could be seen, I open my note book at 4 November 1959 and see the numbers of 74 steam locomotives written there; there would have been a few diesels too, but I would not have made a note of them at this period in my career! This haul of 74 locomotives

Crewe North's best, 46256 SIR WILLIAM A STANIER FRS, at rest at Crewe North on Sunday 27 September 1964. It had worked the RCTS Scottish Lowlander rail tour the previous day in both directions between Crewe and Carlisle. This was not only its last working but also the last for the class – in BR ownership at least. Within a few weeks, along with her remaining sisters at Crewe North (all the working examples had been concentrated there for the last few weeks of use) 46256 had been dispatched for breaking up. Tragic that this one was not saved. The diagonal yellow stripe on the cab side applied early in the summer of 1964 signified that the engine should not work south of Crewe due to its limited clearance under the overhead line electrification equipment, then proceeding south towards London. (JB Bucknall)

included eight Duchesses, two Princesses, eleven Scots, eight Baby Scots, four Jubilees, two Britannias, fifteen Class 5s and two Western Region engines.

Crewe Works annual open days were a must and having usually met one or two other enthusiasts – I recall several lads of about my age were also Saturday morning regulars – we would set off on foot to the Deviation Works entrance in Eaton Street. There, after assembly in groups, we were taken for a wide-ranging tour. Although these escorted tours embraced many of the shops in the Steel Works, as I later knew it, it was the Vacuum and Steam Cleaning pits, and the main Erecting Shop that provided us with the most interest and of course numbers!

I recall they were building the Derby designed and Sulzer engined Type 2s (later Class 24), and the similarly designed and engined Type 4s (later Class 45) but the bulk of what I later knew as 'Ten Shop' was full of steam locomotives undergoing repairs. There were two lots of outside pits, which took their names from their principal purpose. On the Steam Cleaning Pits incoming engines were separated from their tenders and steam cleaned to remove as much muck as possible before they moved to the stripping pits. The Vacuum Pits were where engines were steam tested after overhaul, before going into the Paint Shop. One of the most important jobs was to test the vacuum brake equipment for any air leaking into the system, hence the name of these pits, which were outside the Brass Finishing Shop and just outside the Paint Shop. With all this background then, it was a foregone conclusion that I wanted to be a Railwayman.

If I was not at Crewe, Derby or Wolverhampton, I would cycle the ten miles or so from where we then lived in Newcastle-under-Lyme to be alongside the West Coast Main Line at Stableford, Whitmore or Madeley. If I only had a half day, or it was a summer evening, I would be by the line at Etruria, or Stoke itself.

So then, it came about that I started my career as a Railwayman, a little after my 15th birthday in the early months of 1962, as an apprentice fitter at Crewe North Shed. At this time the Shedmaster at Crewe North was one Geoff Sands, having moved there from Stoke a year or so before. Geoff was quite new to the London Midland Region having trained on the Eastern, and as a native of Norwich had spent much of his time in East Anglia. He had come to Stoke from Melton Constable on the old Midland & Great Northern section; his father, Tom Sands, was a much-respected Headquarters Footplate Inspector at Norwich, having graduated from the footplate. Geoff had done the bulk of his training at Norwich and in Stratford Works.

The south end of Crewe South shed on 8 September 1967 and ex-Crosti boiler 9F 92029, a couple of months before closure to steam. Although a Lancaster Green Ayre shed code is painted on, it was actually a Birkenhead engine at the time, and would have worked to Crewe with iron ore from Bidston Dock for Shelton Steel Works in Stoke-on-Trent. Stoke shed had closed to steam the previous month so Birkenhead 9Fs came off these trains at Crewe and diesels worked forward. Your author can be seen on the left with contemporary David Owen on the right; there is a lead hammer on the buffer beam, but I cannot recall what we had been hitting!

My father was an accomplished model engineer, building live steam locomotives in 2½, 3½ and 5 inch gauges, and we were both keen members of the local North Staffs Models Society – indeed Dad had been a founder member when it was first formed before the war. Among the members were a number of Stoke footplate men, for example the late Jack Lynch, a driver then in the spare link, and the Yates brothers, Dennis and Les, both firemen.

It was not long then before Geoff was introduced to Society members and of course, cajoled into giving a talk on his experiences. Dad and Geoff soon became firm friends as Dad too came from the Fens, having been born and brought up in Huntingdon. One of his engines was a fine scale 3½ inch gauge Great Eastern Railway Claud Hamilton 4-4-0 and the prototypes were favourites of Geoff's. I have this engine now, inheriting it some years ago in the will of a family friend who had purchased it from the fellow Dad sold it to. This sale incidentally, was to help pay for my sister's wedding!

A friend of my mother's from school days was Arthur Cholerton, indeed the two families lived next door to each other. Arthur was a Stoke driver too and, of course, still a family friend, so it was not long before Dad and I used to join Geoff and his Mechanical Foreman Sam Smith, for a few hours on Saturday mornings in and around Stoke shed! Arthur by the way was at this time Chairman of the Stoke footplatemen's

General view of Crewe South shed looking south, and very much as I remember it. This would doubtless be a Sunday, given the number of engines present; the two 3F 0-6-0Ts to the left would otherwise be engaged on shunting duties around the station. The year is 1964 I would say – notice the WR Grange by the coaler which, incidentally, was unique and in part dated back to LNWR times. (Jim Hardy)

LDC (Local Departmental Committee), and went on to a career in local politics becoming in turn Lord Mayor of the City of Stoke-on-Trent, a member of Staffordshire County Council, and subsequently its Chairman.

Obviously after Geoff moved to Crewe we made our Saturday morning visits there, and I was able at last to penetrate that haven of the North Shed, and wander round almost to my heart's content, escorted by Geoff of course. It was Geoff then who was instrumental in the start to my career, advising against my initial inclination towards the footplate, to take an apprenticeship instead. Added to this he recommended that rather than working at Stoke, for the sake of a 25 minute train journey, Crewe would be a better place. This was very sound advice that has stood me in good stead ever since, and before he left for pastures new on the Southern Region he proffered two other good pieces of advice. First, be prepared to move around the country to advance a career and, secondly, develop a skin like a rhinoceros! I have taken both these on board and my career has taken me on to all the old BR Regions, and you certainly needed plenty of hard skin in some of the places I have worked!

Crewe South, 27 October 1967 and Class 5 44759. I am in the centre with Fitter Harry Morton to the left and Leading Fitter Bill Davies, who was acting Mechanical Foreman at the time, to the right.

Crewe South shed, your author on the right with contemporary Chris Jones. We are standing alongside a rather woebegone Class 5, 44759. The date is 27 October 1967, and within a matter of days steam working at Crewe would be over.

The eve of closure to steam at Crewe South, with Class 5 45349 prepared for its next turn of duty. This is the afternoon of 4 November 1967 and the last booked steam workings took place the following day. However, because a number of 'foreign' locomotives were still on shed there was some spasmodic activity the following week as they were gradually worked away. I recall two Carlisle Britannias 'marooned' after working south on the Saturday afternoon, with no immediate balancing workings. And of course, there were a lot of withdrawn locomotives waiting to be hauled away for scrapping. It was well into the following year before they were all cleared.

Princess Royal Pacific 46210 LADY PATRICIA at its home shed of Crewe North on 28 March 1954. A long-term resident of 5A, from 1943 until 1956 (except for a brief loan to the Western Region in February 1956) she is on the preparation roads in the shed yard. The angle of this photograph illustrates perfectly the great size of these well-proportioned locomotives. The Royal Scot to the left is, from its unique nameplate, unmistakably 46127 OLD CONTEMPTIBLES, a Holyhead engine at the time and so well-known at Crewe North. Notice how nice and clean the shed yard is! (AW Battson, The Transport Treasury)

Chapter One
A Railwayman at Last - Life at Crewe North

Some things stay clearly in the memory, for a lifetime, and my first day at work in 1962 is but one of them in my case. I recall going to bed the previous Sunday evening with some trepidation of what the morrow might bring. Mother got me up bright and early the next morning to see me off with haversack packed with my lunch and I walked to Etruria station, about ten minutes away. Taking the train to Crewe, once there I made my way over the footbridge, along No.1 platform and with not a few butterflies in the stomach, over the staff bridge (from where, in train spotting days, we used to watch the trains on the Independent lines) and on to the North Shed. Geoff had told me to knock on his door first which I did, and he took me to his Chief Clerk Fred Cornes who, after the usual formalities which included arrangements for a medical examination later in the week, took me down through that famous tunnel walkway (known as the Gullet) into the depths of the Middle Shed at Crewe North. There I was handed over to Leading Fitter Bill Webb (no relation so far as I am aware to the infamous Francis William!).

Across the end of the shed was a row of engines undergoing repairs or examination of one sort or another, including a few diesels on 2, 3 and 4 roads. What a memorable sight they made, and one that I can see as clearly now as forty-odd years ago. There were two Pacifics facing me on Nos.7 and 8 roads, 46228 DUCHESS OF RUTLAND on No.7 and 46253 CITY OF ST ALBANS on No.8 both, I found out later, undergoing No.8 valve and piston (V&P) examinations. After showing me where to hang my coat and haversack, I put on my overalls and Bill handed me over to the tender mercies of fitter Alf Platt, with whom I was to work for the next few months. Incidentally, we never used the BR '4' in reference to ex-LMS engines, so 46228 and 46253, for instance, were simply 6228 and 6253. For readers' sakes, we'll use the full BR number in these pages.

At this time Alf would have been turned 60, 62 I reckon, and had been a North Shed fitter almost all his working life, although I believe he actually served his time in the Works. In any event he would have entered the service of the LNWR before the First World War, and did not serve in the forces in either that conflict or the later one, as by and large railway craftsman were exempt from military service. Alf had however, in his youth, played professional football for the local team, Crewe Alexandra, or 'The Alex' as it is known, in the days when such an occupation was a part time job to earn some extra money – how times have changed! By this time in his career Alf had a skin ailment due to years of immersing unprotected hands and in oils and greases, and he was engaged on what was termed 'light work' for that reason.

Tradition was, and had been for several years, that Alf had the youngest apprentice with him. Therefore, anything involving heavy lifting or oil and grease was my lot. What became apparent to me very soon, not just from my association with Alf but with other older fitters, was how these men were old before their time. Years of 'mauling' the heavy components of steam locomotives with virtually no mechanical help at all, had taken its toll. Along with many of his contemporaries Alf had a slightly hunched back, well-worn features and extremely hard skin on his hands. All the older blokes were on light work, not usually in any official way but rather by local agreement. Apart from those on Examining Fitter duties, they all had apprentices and/or mates to help them. With very few exceptions, these

Princess Royal 46206 PRINCESS MARIE LOUISE at Crewe North, topping up the tender with water before going off shed to work a train north – notice the well coaled tender. Most enginemen would not miss a last opportunity 'to put the bag in'. Although undated, I would say that this picture was taken at some time between visits to Crewe Works in March 1958 and February 1959. At the former visit it would almost certainly have received the revised BR emblem seen here on the tender, and at the later visit AWS equipment, which it does not have in this illustration. Another long-time 5A resident, it was there from October 1954 until March 1961, although it had been allocated in earlier times too, and returned for a few months in the summer of 1961. (DH Beecroft, The Transport Treasury)

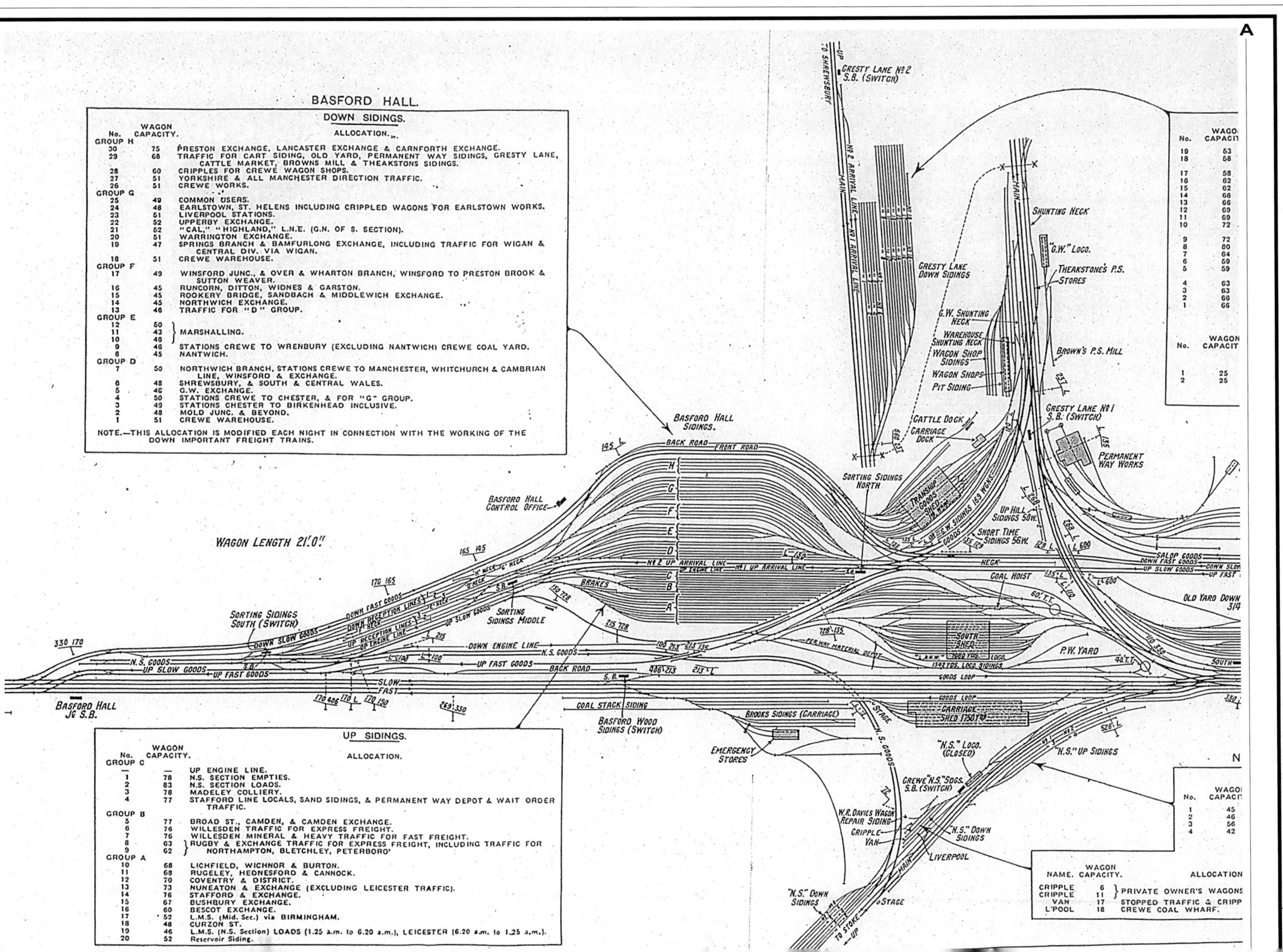

DOWN SIDINGS.

No.	WAGON CAPACITY.	ALLOCATION.
GROUP H		
30	75	PRESTON EXCHANGE, LANCASTER EXCHANGE & CARNFORTH EXCHANGE.
29	68	TRAFFIC FOR CART SIDING, OLD YARD, PERMANENT WAY SIDINGS, GRESTY LANE, CATTLE MARKET, BROWNS MILL & THEAKSTONS SIDINGS.
28	60	CRIPPLES FOR CREWE WAGON SHOPS.
27	51	YORKSHIRE & ALL MANCHESTER DIRECTION TRAFFIC.
26	51	CREWE WORKS.
GROUP G		
25	49	COMMON USERS.
24	48	EARLSTOWN, ST. HELENS INCLUDING CRIPPLED WAGONS FOR EARLSTOWN WORKS.
23	51	LIVERPOOL STATIONS.
22	52	UPPERBY EXCHANGE.
21	52	"CAL," "HIGHLAND," L.N.E. (G.N. OF S. SECTION).
20	51	WARRINGTON EXCHANGE.
19	47	SPRINGS BRANCH & BAMFURLONG EXCHANGE, INCLUDING TRAFFIC FOR WIGAN & CENTRAL DIV. VIA WIGAN.
18	51	CREWE WAREHOUSE.
GROUP F		
17	49	WINSFORD JUNC., & OVER & WHARTON BRANCH, WINSFORD TO PRESTON BROOK & SUTTON WEAVER.
16	45	RUNCORN, DITTON, WIDNES & GARSTON.
15	45	ROOKERY BRIDGE, SANDBACH & MIDDLEWICH EXCHANGE.
14	45	NORTHWICH EXCHANGE.
13	46	TRAFFIC FOR "D" GROUP.
GROUP E		
12	50	} MARSHALLING.
11	43	} MARSHALLING.
10	48	} MARSHALLING.
9	46	STATIONS CREWE TO WRENBURY (EXCLUDING NANTWICH) CREWE COAL YARD.
8	45	NANTWICH.
GROUP D		
7	50	NORTHWICH BRANCH, STATIONS CREWE TO MANCHESTER, WHITCHURCH & CAMBRIAN LINE, WINSFORD & EXCHANGE.
6	48	SHREWSBURY, & SOUTH & CENTRAL WALES.
5	46	G.W. EXCHANGE.
4	50	STATIONS CREWE TO CHESTER, & FOR "G" GROUP.
3	49	STATIONS CHESTER TO BIRKENHEAD INCLUSIVE.
2	48	MOLD JUNC. & BEYOND.
1	51	CREWE WAREHOUSE.

NOTE.—THIS ALLOCATION IS MODIFIED EACH NIGHT IN CONNECTION WITH THE WORKING OF THE DOWN IMPORTANT FREIGHT TRAINS.

UP SIDINGS.

No.	WAGON CAPACITY.	ALLOCATION.
GROUP C		
—	—	UP ENGINE LINE.
1	78	N.S. SECTION EMPTIES.
2	83	N.S. SECTION LOADS.
3	78	MADELEY COLLIERY.
4	77	STAFFORD LINE LOCALS, SAND SIDINGS, & PERMANENT WAY DEPOT & WAIT ORDER TRAFFIC.
GROUP B		
5	77	BROAD ST., CAMDEN, & CAMDEN EXCHANGE.
6	76	WILLESDEN TRAFFIC FOR EXPRESS FREIGHT.
7	76	WILLESDEN MINERAL & HEAVY TRAFFIC FOR FAST FREIGHT.
8	63	} RUGBY & EXCHANGE TRAFFIC FOR EXPRESS FREIGHT, INCLUDING TRAFFIC FOR NORTHAMPTON, BLETCHLEY, PETERBORO'
9	62	} RUGBY & EXCHANGE TRAFFIC FOR EXPRESS FREIGHT, INCLUDING TRAFFIC FOR NORTHAMPTON, BLETCHLEY, PETERBORO'
GROUP A		
10	68	LICHFIELD, WICHNOR & BURTON.
11	68	RUGELEY, HEDNESFORD & CANNOCK.
12	70	COVENTRY & DISTRICT.
13	73	NUNEATON & EXCHANGE (EXCLUDING LEICESTER TRAFFIC).
14	76	STAFFORD & EXCHANGE.
15	67	BUSHBURY EXCHANGE.
16	60	BESCOT EXCHANGE.
17	52	L.M.S. (Mid. Sec.) via BIRMINGHAM.
18	48	CURZON ST.
19	46	L.M.S. (N.S. Section) LOADS (1.25 a.m. to 6.20 a.m.), LEICESTER (6.20 a.m. to 1.25 a.m.).
20	52	Reservoir Siding.

No.	WAGO[N] CAPACIT[Y]
19	53
18	58
17	58
16	62
15	62
14	66
13	66
12	69
11	69
10	72
9	72
8	80
7	64
6	59
5	59
4	63
3	63
2	68
1	66

No.	WAGON CAPACIT[Y]
1	25
2	25

No.	WAGO[N] CAPACI[TY]
1	45
2	46
3	56
4	42

NAME.	WAGON CAPACITY.	ALLOCATION
CRIPPLE	6	} PRIVATE OWNER'S WAGONS
CRIPPLE	11	} PRIVATE OWNER'S WAGONS
VAN	17	STOPPED TRAFFIC & CRIPP
L'POOL	18	CREWE COAL WHARF.

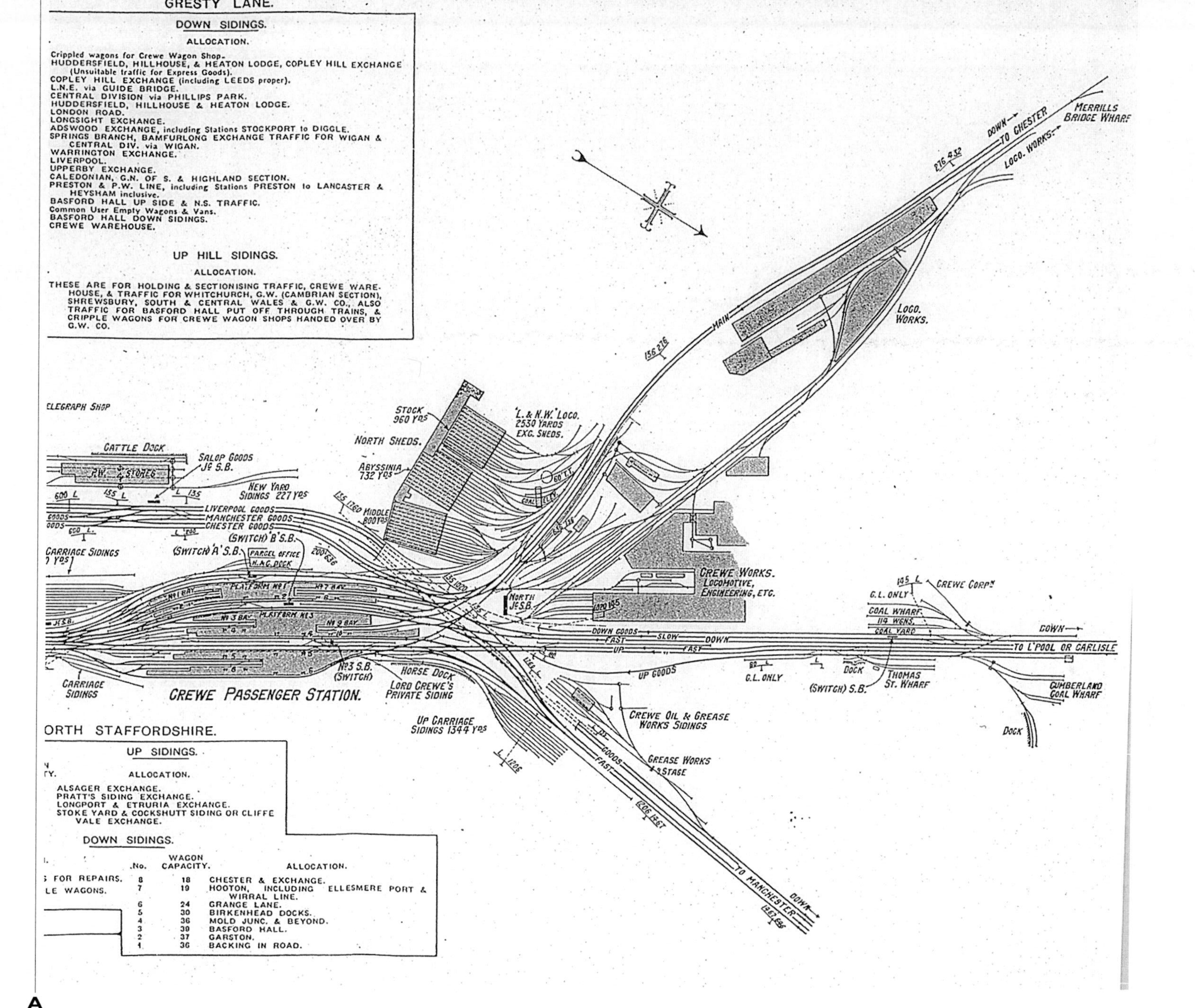

GRESTY LANE.

DOWN SIDINGS.

ALLOCATION.

Crippled wagons for Crewe Wagon Shop.
HUDDERSFIELD, HILLHOUSE, & HEATON LODGE, COPLEY HILL EXCHANGE (Unsuitable traffic for Express Goods).
COPLEY HILL EXCHANGE (including LEEDS proper).
L.N.E. via GUIDE BRIDGE.
CENTRAL DIVISION via PHILLIPS PARK.
HUDDERSFIELD, HILLHOUSE & HEATON LODGE.
LONDON ROAD.
LONGSIGHT EXCHANGE.
ADSWOOD EXCHANGE, including Stations STOCKPORT to DIGGLE.
SPRINGS BRANCH, BAMFURLONG EXCHANGE TRAFFIC FOR WIGAN & CENTRAL DIV. via WIGAN.
WARRINGTON EXCHANGE.
LIVERPOOL.
UPPERBY EXCHANGE.
CALEDONIAN, G.N. OF S. & HIGHLAND SECTION.
PRESTON & P.W. LINE, including Stations PRESTON to LANCASTER & HEYSHAM inclusive.
BASFORD HALL UP SIDE & N.S. TRAFFIC.
Common User Empty Wagons & Vans.
BASFORD HALL DOWN SIDINGS.
CREWE WAREHOUSE.

UP HILL SIDINGS.

ALLOCATION.

THESE ARE FOR HOLDING & SECTIONISING TRAFFIC, CREWE WAREHOUSE, & TRAFFIC FOR WHITCHURCH, G.W. (CAMBRIAN SECTION), SHREWSBURY, SOUTH & CENTRAL WALES & G.W. CO., ALSO TRAFFIC FOR BASFORD HALL PUT OFF THROUGH TRAINS, & CRIPPLE WAGONS FOR CREWE WAGON SHOPS HANDED OVER BY G.W. CO.

ORTH STAFFORDSHIRE.

UP SIDINGS.

ALLOCATION.

ALSAGER EXCHANGE.
PRATT'S SIDING EXCHANGE.
LONGPORT & ETRURIA EXCHANGE.
STOKE YARD & COCKSHUTT SIDING OR CLIFFE VALE EXCHANGE.

DOWN SIDINGS.

	No.	WAGON CAPACITY.	ALLOCATION.
; FOR REPAIRS.	8	18	CHESTER & EXCHANGE.
LE WAGONS.	7	19	HOOTON, INCLUDING ELLESMERE PORT & WIRRAL LINE.
	6	24	GRANGE LANE.
	5	30	BIRKENHEAD DOCKS.
	4	36	MOLD JUNC. & BEYOND.
	3	39	BASFORD HALL.
	2	37	GARSTON.
	1	36	BACKING IN ROAD.

A

Rebuilt Patriot 45523 BANGOR, under the coaling plant at Crewe North in March 1954. A Camden engine at the time and clearly 'ex-works' – 'fresh off' in Crewe parlance. According to the Irwell Press bible on this class of locomotive, the engine history card records a heavy general repair at Crewe between 24 February and 25 March that year. This was a Camden engine for almost ten years between 1951 and 1961, when it went north a mile or so to Willesden, finishing its days from that shed in March 1964. Notice the narrow gauge track in the foreground, used for the ash skips. (AW Battson, The Transport Treasury)

splendid guys did not live long in their well-earned retirement.

One of Alf's jobs was servicing piston valves and I seemed to impress Bill Webb as we walked past Alf on our way to the Fitters Cabin by commenting on the piston valves. "Oh, you know what those are then" he retorted – at least I think I impressed him! To his great credit Geoff had made no mention of our personal relationship, and he treated me like any other member of staff whenever our paths crossed, which was not very often I hasten to add, and I likewise showed no outward signs. Dad had advised me on this issue!

Alf was a super guy, a chain smoker of Woodbines which never seemed to leave his mouth, and made his speech rather difficult to understand at first. But we became firm friends as he showed me all the ropes of working in a Motive Power Depot. And there were more ropes to be shown at Crewe North then most others, with its numerous traditions and foibles, nooks and crannies and the like. Indeed we remained friends until he retired some two or three years later.

My first job was to help overhaul the four piston valves from 46253, which had arrived for its No.8 V&P examination the previous evening, a Sunday, so that work could commence the following day. This, I was to learn later, was the normal practice with these engines so that the day shift could commence work as soon as they booked on, on Monday mornings. By the time I started all four valves were already on the bench, and Alf showed me how to first of all get them hot with twin gas

The North shed yard on 15 October 1949; right is the old LNWR coaling plant with the new reinforced concrete BR one under construction to the left. The old plant dated from 1909 and was the first fully mechanised coaling plant in this country – the skip hoist arrangement can be seen in front of it. The circular apparatus by the bottom of the hoist was the wagon tippler which up-ended wagons so that the coal went into skips beneath to be hoisted into the bunker. Beyond the old plant, and on both sides of it, can just be seen the brick retaining walls of an even earlier coaling stage.

Class 3F 0-6-0T 47505, allocated to Crewe Works when this photograph was taken on 18 August 1963, on the Works 'W1' shunting trip. This was the trip that conveyed Works traffic to and from Basford Hall Marshalling Yard, twice a day, one in the morning and another in the late afternoon. The second conveyed the stores vans with material for the outstation sheds, spares and so on, for marshalling into overnight trains. This very often afforded delivery for UVS (Urgent Vehicle Standing) material the day after it was ordered. Quite often a heavy duty, it more often at this time employed a 'Standard Freight' 4F 0-6-0. Behind the engine is Crewe North's 'Middle Shed' with the Stores building to its left. The platform where the man is standing had a hand-worked hoist for heavy items out of wagons below. To the extreme left are the offices, housing the District Locomotive Superintendent and the Shed Master among others. The oil barrels to the right are for diesel engine lubricating oil. (Ashley Archive, Alan Robinson)

burners so as to loosen as much of the built up carbon as possible. In the process the old rings were removed and the heads then cleaned and examined for any fractures before fitting new rings. The new rings came in one standard size, and were continuous. First then, we had to establish the size of the valve liners using a set of inside callipers. We then cut the ring with a saw, subsequently removing a section so that when the ring was passed along the valve liners, a small gap remained. It was then necessary to file semi-circular notches in each end, so the ring would fit around the spigot that prevented the rings moving round the valve head once in position.

Because the rear valve head was slightly smaller then the front one, to allow easier fitting when passing the rear head through the front liner, an expanding spider-like contraption was used to measure the diameter of the rear liner.

I was then shown how to pack the rings with bits of Alf's old Woodbine packets so as to wedge them compressed, thus easing the job of refitting the valve to the engine – the cardboard would immediately disintegrate as soon as the steam hit it, thus allowing the rings to take up their intended position. The No.8 V&P was the largest of all the examinations undertaken at the LM 'Concentration' Motive Power Depots (the 'A' District sheds) and as well as a couple of Pacifics there would be at least two other engines undergoing similar work at any one time. Nos.7 and 8 roads were always reserved for the Pacifics, with other engines dealt with on 5 and 6 roads. While fitting staff usually referred to the Pacifics as Class 8s, the footplate men more often used either 'Lizzie' for the Princess Royal class, or 'Big Lizzie' for the Duchesses. More frequently they were all just 'Big 'Uns', which of course, by the standards of all the other engines they were!

Irrespective of their home depots, for almost the whole of their lives the Stanier Pacifics came to Crewe North for No.8 V&P examinations. An

The stores at the south-east corner of the Middle Shed, 10 March 1960. The hand-worked jib crane can be seen along with wagons waiting unloading; the barrels contain diesel locomotive lubricating oil. There was no mechanised means for filling the sumps of the diesels at Crewe North and sand buckets (suitably cleaned I hasten to add) were used, placed in the pit with the barrels rolled to the sides.

Top. **Offices and stores, 10 March 1960. The top floor windows of the offices are of a later style than the lower ones, indicating that the top half was an addition. To the left of the bike sheds is the cutting taking the Independent lines under the North Junction – notice the smoke from a passing engine.**

Middle. **The entrance to Crewe North MPD from the station side, looking towards Station Street, March 1960. The Middle Shed Stores is to the right and the white painted arch is the famous foot tunnel into the shed itself, known as the 'Gullet'. Observe the LNWR war memorial plaque prominent on the corner of the office building; in my time this was always highly polished. It now resides in the Drivers' Booking On Point at Crewe Station; there was a similar plaque at the South shed but I don't know where that one went on closure of the shed. Does anybody?**

Bottom. **The unimposing shed entrance from the Station Street side, in March 1960. The doorway with its gantry crane for loading and unloading road vehicles led into the Machine Shop of the Middle Shed. The barrow was of the type used by the Brick Arch Men, for moving arch bricks and other associated material around the shed. The few cars and vacant parking space are testament that few men came to work by these means in those days! Behind the wall to the left is the 'Abyssinia' shed.**

exception came about after nationalisation, Scottish Region engines instead having the work done at Polmadie. The idea behind the policy of concentrating the work at Crewe had been to increase utilisation, for the proximity of Crewe North shed to the Works meant that if any components needed attention there, it could be accomplished quickly. The theory was for the engines to be stopped for the minimum time for the examination, a week being the objective. It was essential to get any parts needing works attention backwards and forwards very quickly. They were transported to and from the Works by road motor.

Such parts on the Duchesses included the rocking levers, which actuated the inside valves from the outside valve gear. They often required rebushing, and along with the lighter motion parts with needle roller bearings, were all jobs we sent to the Works. As a small diversion I might mention one occasion when Alf and I accompanied the lorry to the Works stores to give instructions for a special job of some sort or other, although I cannot now remember exactly what it was. As there was only room for two passengers in the cab, I travelled in the open rear, and on the way back part of the load was a piston and rod. Now this item was not secured so it rolled around in a completely random manner with the movement of the lorry,

Stanier Pacific 46250 CITY OF LICHFIELD in the embryonic semi-roundhouse in 1959. To the left are the remains of 'Abba'; the wall on the right was once the rear of the 'Cage', and the building behind with the windows is part of the *Queens Hotel* in Station Street. (Late George Wheeler)

and I spent all my time moving around too, to avoid it. I could see Alf and the driver, through the rear cab window, laughing and although they denied it, I swear to this day they did it on purpose because whenever again I saw pistons in lorries they were always secured! The No.8 V&P examinations on the Pacifics at Crewe continued until the engines' demise, and the very last one was not undertaken at Crewe North until August 1964, on 6251 CITY OF NOTTINGHAM. The engine never turned another wheel under her own steam, the decision having been taken meantime to withdraw all remaining members of the class at the end of the 1964 summer timetable service.

Alf taught me lots of other things; how to make a steam tight joint, how to re-cut a valve seat, how to use a hammer and chisel with out hitting ones knuckles, how to make a bearing run cool and how to swing a 14lb hammer. I have to say I never fully mastered the latter, but it was an essential part of maintaining steam locomotives, especially in V&P examinations. There were no torque spanners in those days; all nuts and bolts were flogged up by hammers of varying weights depending on the size of bolt or nut; wedges and cotters likewise. The Pacifics usually 'came apart' quite easily as their V&P examinations, at 30-36,000 miles, were due every 12-14 weeks. Other engines, like Class 5s, took far longer to accumulate such mileages and could be real swines. Parts had much more time to 'seize' and would require literally hours of 'flogging' to remove crosshead cotters for example, and then split the taper between crosshead and piston rod. There were some real masters of the big hammer craft at the North Shed, and a sort of hierarchy existed in asking for assistance, so that you did not go and ask those with the highest reputations for shifting recalcitrant cotters, until the lesser brethren had been (literally, sometimes) exhausted! But there was always a great sprit of comradeship and everybody would

Rear of the new semi-roundhouse, almost complete on 14 October 1959. A light and airy building in complete contrast to the earlier sheds, and indeed the remaining Middle Shed. The tracks with sleeper crossing are on ground formerly occupied by the Stock Shed and were used for coal wagons.

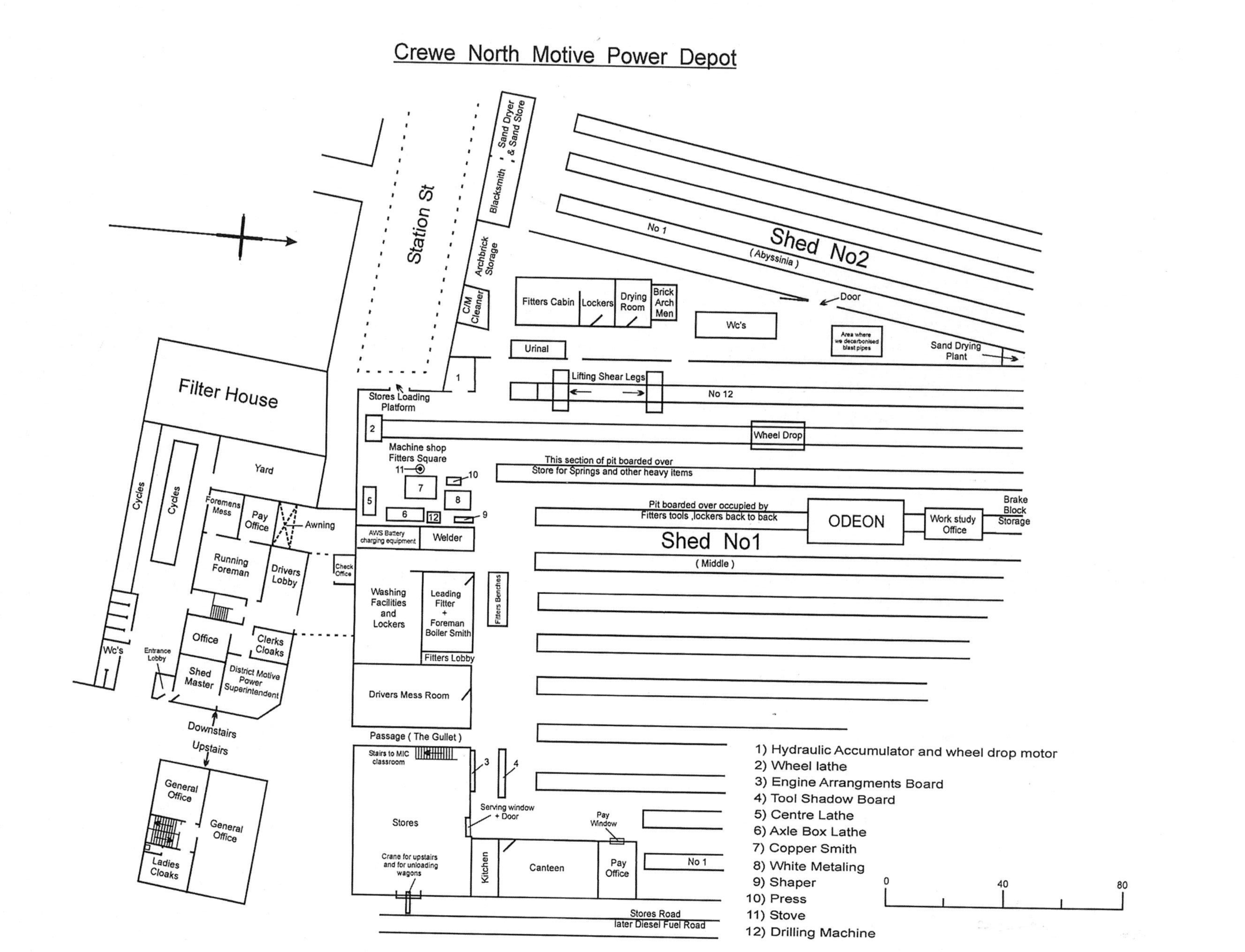
Crewe North Motive Power Depot
Station St
Sand Dryer & Sand Store
Blacksmith
Archbrick Storage
C/M Cleaner
Shed No2
(Abyssinia)
No 1
Door
Fitters Cabin
Lockers
Drying Room
Brick Arch Men
Wc's
Area where we decarbonised blast pipes
Sand Drying Plant
Urinal
Lifting Shear Legs
No 12
Stores Loading Platform
Wheel Drop
Machine shop Fitters Square
This section of pit boarded over
Store for Springs and other heavy items
Pit boarded over occupied by
Fitters tools ,lockers back to back
ODEON
Work study Office
Brake Block Storage
Shed No1
(Middle)
AWS Battery charging equipment
Welder
Filter House
Yard
Cycles
Foremens Mess
Pay Office
Awning
Running Foreman
Drivers Lobby
Check Office
Washing Facilities and Lockers
Leading Fitter + Foreman Boiler Smith
Fitters Benches
Fitters Lobby
Office
Clerks Cloaks
Wc's
Entrance Lobby
Shed Master
District Motive Power Superintendent
Drivers Mess Room
Passage (The Gullet)
Downstairs
Upstairs
General Office
General Office
Ladies Cloaks
Stairs to MIC classroom
Stores
Serving window + Door
Pay Window
Kitchen
Canteen
Pay Office
No 1
Crane for upstairs and for unloading wagons
Stores Road
later Diesel Fuel Road
1) Hydraulic Accumulator and wheel drop motor
2) Wheel lathe
3) Engine Arrangments Board
4) Tool Shadow Board
5) Centre Lathe
6) Axle Box Lathe
7) Copper Smith
8) White Metaling
9) Shaper
10) Press
11) Stove
12) Drilling Machine
0
40
80

Two long-term Crewe North residents outside the Middle Shed on 22 August 1948. These are Webb 5ft 6in 2-4-2 passenger side tanks, a design dating from 1890, many of which were converted to work 'Motor Trains', that is push pull working with the engine remaining at the same end of the train. Both these two were thus converted, evident from the twin vacuum pipes on the buffer beam of the leading engine, still as LMS 6710. It was built at Crewe in February 1895 as LNWR 626 and withdrawn for scrapping in September 1949. Sister engine behind, whilst still retaining LMS insignia, is already renumbered into the BR series with the addition of the 4. This one was built at Crewe in September 1893 as LNWR 2141, becoming LMS 6680, and later BR 46680 – it was not withdrawn until February 1953, remaining allocated to Crewe North until the end. These engines were on the allocation for the 'Motor Trains' to and from Northwich via Middlewich, and when not so employed one would be found on the 'Rag Mail'. (FW Shuttleworth)

muck in if one was in trouble. There is a Crewe term which I had not heard before, and I have never heard it anywhere else since, of being 'straight up'. This in Crewe parlance means finished for the day, and if one was 'straight up' and others were not, then it would be all hands to the grindstone until we were all – 'straight up'! Working with Alf entailed more than piston valve overhaul and a few associated jobs, and whilst we did not work on the mileage examinations we did have a staple diet of 'X' day examinations, together with 3-5 and 7-9 weeks exams, and of course any of the lighter jobs arising. I worked on all the types of engine allocated to Crewe North; as well as the Pacifics there were Royal Scots and Jubilees (we called them either 5XPs or 'Red 'Uns', for when they were new they were painted red, as opposed to the Black 5s, which were always black and known as 'Black 'Uns'). There were also Patriots (we called them Baby Scots, except the rebuilt ones which were known as Scots like their Royal sisters),

Successors to the Webb tanks for the Northwich line services were Ivatt Class 2 2-6-2Ts, also 'Motor' fitted. The vacuum controlled regulator gear can be seen on the side of the smoke box of 41229, outside the Middle Shed on 5 May 1963. These engines also participated in working the 'Rag Mail' and continued to do so until the shed closed. Incidentally, in my time despite the fact the Northwich branch had lost its passenger service a couple of years earlier, we continued to maintain the push-pull control gear although it was never used! (Mike Fell).

'Motor' fitted Ivatt tank 41215 in ex-works condition on the coaling road at Crewe North, 20 August 1959. The vacuum controlled regulator gear is very clear in this view – the white vacuum pipe is the control one, painted thus to distinguish it for train crews and shunters. A Chester Northgate locomotive at this time it would be awaiting return to its home depot – there were at the period a number of 'Motor' diagrams from that shed.

Class 5s, and the small assortment of other engines. These included three long-term residents, Ivatt Class 2 2-6-2 tanks 41212, 41220 and 41229 and these shared duties on the line via Sandbach to Northwich as well as working the 'Rag Mail'. All three were 'motor fitted' so as to be able to work the push-pull trains that had operated the Crewe to Northwich passenger service until this ceased about 1960, but a parcels service survived. The 'Rag Mail' was the term used for one of the local trip workings which largely consisting of shunting the locomotive material stores vans around, the locomotive coal, diesel fuel tankers and other similar duties.

There were also two Fairburn Class 4 2-6-4 tanks, 42079 and 42100 and these as far as I recall, worked between Chester and Whitchurch. We had BR Standard 2MT 2-6-0 78030 which seemed to be reserved for working 'Officers' specials'. It was, accordingly, kept in immaculate condition and when not so used, was utilised as the shed pilot. By this time George Dow, whose name and exploits will be known to many readers, was the Divisional Manager at Stoke-on-Trent, and his area covered Crewe. Hence this engine was used on his saloon regularly; he always seemed to be off somewhere but then the Stoke Division was a large one geographically and at the time many of the branches were under threat. I am sure, being the enthusiast he was, George would have been anxious to travel over them all as a sort of pre-closure inspection! Later, as the Scots were withdrawn, we got an ever-increasing allocation of Britannias, and of course we had the solitary BR Class 8, 71000 DUKE OF GLOUCESTER, which I worked on a couple of times. This engine was however, withdrawn only a few months after I started work.

Crewe North was a truly amazing place in those days; there had been three 12 road sheds of which only one, the Middle Shed (dating from 1865) survived intact by this time. It got its name from the fact that there had been another shed to its east, demolished in the turn of the century remodelling works, which both extended the station and created the Independent lines. As a part of the post-war remodelling of Crewe North, much of the shed to the west of the Middle Shed, known as 'Abyssinia' (always abbreviated to 'Abba', it was so named as it dated from the time of one of the Abyssinian wars in 1868) had been largely demolished. The westernmost four roads of 'Abba'

Stanier Mogul 42958 at the North shed on 20 August 1959. It was actually allocated then – a few were at Crewe North about this time, but not for very long. The engine is standing on No.4 road of what remained there at 'Abyssinia' shed; notice the edge of the new turntable pit in the foreground.

A Duchess Pacific looking to be just off an intermediate repair in the Works and doubtless waiting its first job. This is a long-time Edge Hill resident 46241 CITY OF EDINBURGH, at Crewe North about 1959. (Late George Wheeler)

were shorter than the others by about one engine's length and for some reason I know not, were called the Cage. The third shed was known as the Stock Shed; dating from 1891-92, its principal use was the storage of out of service engines. It had been completely demolished and its site part-occupied by a 12 road semi-roundhouse, which was all that was built of an otherwise comprehensive post-war remodelling scheme. This scheme was to have embraced two complete roundhouses. Almost all the repair and examination work was undertaken in the Middle Shed, although some of the smaller examinations were undertaken in Abba, or what was left of it, with the roundhouse largely occupied by engines in steam and between jobs.

The Middle Shed had all the equipment required of a 'Concentration Depot' as defined in the 1932 LMS 'Motive Power Area Locomotive Supply, Repair, Concentration & Garage Scheme' and included a large machine shop. Here was to be found a wheel lathe, axle box lathe, medium sized centre lathe, shaper, drilling machines and so on, along with facilities for a coppersmith and tinsmith, for white metalling bearings and sundry other jobs. The blacksmith's shop was at the southern end of what remained of Abba, along with a covered area for the storage of arch bricks and other large items.

It was the practice to try and keep some of the LMR Pacifics at particular sheds for long periods of time where there were connections with the engine's names. Thus 46238 CITY OF CARLISLE was a long-term resident of the Carlisle sheds, either Upperby or Kingmoor; in this view she bears an Upperby shed plate (12B). The engine is in the later maroon livery and is standing on the 'going off road', so is doubtless waiting for the signal to move off to the station to pick up her next working. (Late George Wheeler)

From the seemingly low amount of coal in the tender it would appear that 46236 CITY OF BRADFORD is coming onto the shed on completion of a job. A picture taken about 1958. (Late George Wheeler)

George Burton was the jovial Coppersmith, Ernie Hilditch the Blacksmith, and Bob Colclough Ernie's mate.

Of the roads in the Middle Shed No.1 and 2 were much truncated as a canteen and pay office had been built at its southern end – what was left of No.1 usually housed the 50 ton breakdown crane (No.RS 1005/50 Cowans Sheldon 1930, uprated from 36 tons in the early years of the War) which was kept in steam all the time. No.3 road was also shortened, but only by about half an engine's length, to allow men to move around the canteen and pay office. Nos.2-4 roads were by this time largely used by the diesels.

The southern end of roads 5, 6, 7 and 8 were used for locomotives undergoing V&P examinations; 7 and 8 were reserved for the Pacifics, with other examination and repair work going on behind them. No.9 road had been completely severed, and instead housed at its mid-length the Mechanical Foreman and Shed Clerks offices, one above the other and known as the 'Odeon' – this would presumably date its construction as the mid-1930s. In front of this at the southern end were the fitters' tool lockers, and behind it the work study office and a storage area for yet more heavy items including arch bricks, fire bars, brake blocks and the like. The next road westwards, No.10, was also severed but in this case only for its southern half, the pit being boarded over and used to store laminated bearing springs and yet more heavy items too bulky to go in the Stores. No.11 had the wheel drop half way along its length; this road extended into the machine shop and at its extreme end was the wheel lathe.

On No.12 there was a rather antiquated set of shear legs, which in earlier days lifted the lighter locomotives bodily to remove wheel sets. I only ever saw this apparatus used to lift some of the South Shed 3F shunting tanks, which would be sent over if ever they required lifting. Like the wheel drop the lifting mechanism was hydraulically operated and there was a large hydraulic accumulator at the southern end of the Middle Shed, with associated electrically operated pump etc. Also at this end were the stores, a large two story building at the south-east corner.

In order, moving west across the southern end of the shed from the stores, was the footplatemen's mess room (devoid, incidentally, of any natural light), Fitters' Lobby, Leading Fitter and Boilersmith's office, rudimentary washing facilities and the lockers (these were actually behind the Leading Fitter's Office) and then the Machine Shop. Between all this and the end of the roads were fitters' benches, engine arrangements board and a 'shadow' board on which were located a vast assortment of heavy tools and equipment. This part of the Middle Shed was very much the centre of activities, but it was all rather decrepit with much of the roof at least partly missing. When it rained you knew about it and though there was a welcoming stove in the Machine Shop, like all steam sheds of course, it was without proper heating of any sort, except hot water or coals from a handy locomotive!

Outside the Middle Shed on its east (that is, the station) side, there were two roads. The outer one served the stores and extended to an area south of the shed, passing in front of the main offices buildings to the Outdoor Machinery Department workshops. The other road, alongside the shed wall, had been adapted for fuelling and watering diesel locomotives, with a fuelling plant erected there. Another road branched off the one serving the stores and continued parallel to the No.1 through road of the station, alongside the cutting carrying the Independent lines, to terminate by the bridge carrying the Nantwich Road over the railway. This was known, for some reason I have never been able to fathom, as 'Welsh's Siding, and here the breakdown train was stabled. When there was a call for the train an engine would be attached to the crane in No.1 road, and after drawing it out of the shed it would be propelled on to the train in 'Welsh's Siding, before setting off for wherever it was going. If it was heading south, the engine would run round at the shed exit, or another one would be attached at the southern end. It was the proud boast of the North Shed that, at any time of the day or night, this train could be on its way in 45 minutes and as this often included calling men out from their homes, it was no mean achievement.

The fuel storage tanks were located right at the opposite side of the shed, alongside what had been the westernmost wall of the Stock Shed, and the 60,000 gallon water storage tank was there too. There were also facilities at this side of the shed, for discharging rail tank wagons, as well as several roads for stabling loaded and empty locomotive coal wagons.

At this time the Mechanical Foreman was Bill Short – for some reason always known as Tom – who had come to Crewe from Leeds Holbeck. The other two Leading Fitters sharing the three shifts with Bill Webb were Tommy Brooks and Burt Ashwin – both Crewe North men for their entire careers. There was also a Foreman Boilersmith, Charlie Farr, who looked after the entire Crewe Motive Power District; he was thus out and about a lot. In view of the importance of achieving a quick turnaround with the Pacifics, there was a separate 'Under Mechanical Foreman' on a day turn for this work. In my time Joe Lee was 'acting' in this position as the 'permanent' occupant Jack Lawton, was on extended sick leave – I don't remember him myself. Nevertheless, he had a tremendous reputation! Moving up a few rungs, the District Motive Power Superintendent (who had his offices at Crewe North) was Norman Peach, and his assistant was Tom Vickers, who himself had started his career as an apprentice at Crewe North.

When I graduated up from working with Alf (who incidentally went to keep a boarding house in Blackpool on retirement, though I never heard of him again) I worked with a variety of fitters and on all sorts of jobs. Mileage examinations now came my way as well as work on engines in steam, 'Y' scheme as it was called, as opposed to 'X' scheme. The term 'X' day was used under the aforementioned LMS scheme of 1932; for the want of a better term it designated the day a locomotive would be stopped for routine examination. This took place at either 7-day intervals (express passenger locomotives) or 14-day intervals (all other types) when the opportunity would also be taken to undertake any other examinations due, for example V&P, 3-5 week or 7-9 week exam. It naturally followed, at least at Crewe that is, that any other work would be 'Y' work, or as it was called at Crewe 'Wise'. The 'X' scheme philosophy was extended to the entire BR system, for by and large it was ex-LMS Motive Power men who took over the Headquarters Department, but I never heard the 'Y' scheme term used anywhere else I worked!

I spent quite a lot of time with Stan Nichols; he was just turned 20 and had been 'made up' as it was termed, working as a fitter for the last years of his apprenticeship. This was normal practice with Motive Power apprentices at Crewe, and indeed many other depots and had the effect of not only giving early experience of the responsibilities of a fitter, but also reduced the pay bill! Such apprentices only worked a day turn, and the Leading Fitters were required to extend an increased level of supervision, but in my experience then, and later in my own case, this was in sprit rather than practice! However, part of the philosophy was that those 'made up' had much of the heavy work to do, allowing older men to undertake 'light work'. So it was that we did plenty of mileage exams on anything but the Pacifics, because these engines (as we saw earlier) had dedicated gangs allocated to them. We got the Scots, 'Red 'Uns' and the like, and occasionally had jobs on the wheel drop, but as this work was usually undertaken 'on days' by the resident men of the breakdown gang, we only got this type of work if the breakdown gang were out on a job – which I have to say they frequently were.

Young apprentices used to get up to all sorts of tricks! My contemporary was Peter Scarrat whose father was a driver, and who had started but a few weeks before me. In general terms the Crewe Motive Power area took on two apprentices each year and so I soon got to know the others, of which Stan and Sid Ollier were in their last year and working as Fitters. Sid's father was also a driver, nicknamed Bud, he was a well-known Crewe character and for many years in the No.2, Perth link – he was reckoned to be the only driver who would take 71000 DUKE OF GLOUCESTER to Perth without complaining! When work was done and we were all 'straight up', among the things we used to get up to was playing football behind the semi roundhouse (sometimes against the engine cleaners who we always beat!) and I recall one day being almost caught, or so we thought, by the Leading Fitter, in this case the infamous Tommy Brooks. We fled, unfortunately leaving the ball behind in the process but Tommy had seen and recognised at least one of us and of course, he took

Very long-term Crewe North resident 46235 CITY OF BIRMINGHAM, outside the Middle Shed in July 1962. This engine was allocated to Crewe for almost its entire working life, and is currently preserved in Birmingham. She stars in Chapter Four. (Late George Wheeler)

Princess Royal Pacific 46203 PRINCESS MARGARET ROSE waiting to leave the North shed for its next job. She was allocated to Crewe North between May 1953 and October 1958; the later BR emblem on the tender would indicate a picture taken nearer the latter date. For long periods Crewe North had several 'Lizzies' on its books. In the background can be seen a 'Midland' 2P on a train from North Wales, presumably awaiting the signal to enter the station.

charge of the ball – a treasured item that had been handed down through a succession of North Shed apprentices and over many years! Later that afternoon – I think it must have been a lunch time game in this particular instance – by which time we assumed we had got away with it, we were summoned to see the Mechanical Foreman, one Albert Mee. We solemnly made our way up the steps to his office on the top deck of the 'Odeon'. There we were 'dealt' with in no uncertain terms, and on leaving with tails between legs, Albert said 'aren't you forgetting something', and handed us back our beloved ball – we would have been even more severely dealt with by our colleagues if we had lost it! Albert Mee by the way had replaced 'Tom' Short, and came to Crewe from Longsight. He later went on to become Breakdown Foreman when this was made a permanent position and retired from that post at Crewe Diesel Depot in November 1978. Albert was LNER trained, at Gorton, and for his work with the breakdown gang he was in 1976 awarded the British Empire Medal, by the then Lord Lieutenant of Cheshire.

We used to get up to all sorts of other tricks, and of course there was a ritual of inducting new starters, tricks like putting the 'bags' into tender tanks and turning the water on when the victim was inside! Part of the 7-9 week schedule was an examination of the inside of the tender tanks, removing scale, and checking the working of the tank water level gauge – a job for apprentices if ever there was one. 'Bag', incidentally, was a Crewe term for a water column 'hose' and it took me some time to realise this when people kept talking about them! Hence the enginemen's term, 'put the bag in'. It came from the much earlier use of leather for hosepipes and of course, leather was used for the locomotive water column hoses.

Having smoke box doors slammed shut when one was working inside was another trick, followed by lighting a fire of oily rags in the firebox. Fortunately I was quite slim in those days and I could generally extract myself up the chimney before the fire caught hold; others more portly could not! In earlier days there was a 'standard' trick played against new entrants, or so I was told. Between 'Abba' and the Stock Shed there were two roads where loaded coal wagons were kept, such that they could gravitate to the mechanical coaling plant when needed; over the top there was a sprinkler system to help lay the dust on the coal before it was tipped. Now here lurked the 'Ghost of Abyssinia', or so the unsuspecting were told. Anyway, at a suitable time and after dark, newcomers were told to wait in an appointed spot and they would see the Ghost – in fact of course, the sprinkler system was turned on above them!

In winter it was a very cold place to work, especially if the engine we were working on was stabled in the open in what was left of Abba. In these cases we would first get a couple of braziers, one on each side of the engine and with firelighters from the stores and coal from the tenders, a couple of blazing infernos would soon be under way. As we worked our way through the examination and repairs we would keep stopping for a warm – two pairs of overalls would be the norm on such days, one on top of the other.

Thinking back it was quite dangerous what we used to have to do, as there was no staging of any sort and repairing steam pipe joints, servicing the vacuum ejector and similar jobs entailed working on the foot framing of the engine. An even worse prospect was the top of the boiler, attending to feed clacks and regulators with no support except to cling to the handrails. And of course, in frosty weather these would be very, very cold. This was especially dangerous on the BR Standard designs, as so much of the equipment was strung on the boiler; ex-LMS engines had much of it in the cab. But we never bothered about such niceties, and I do not recall any serious accidents like falling off an engine. If our arch enemies (in a nice sort of way that is!) the Boiler Washers were doing their job at the same time as ours, then the whole place was smothered with running water, and the pit would soon fill up with the scale coming out of the boiler making it impossible to get underneath the engine from one end to the other! These blokes were a breed on their own, messed in separate 'home made' facilities and used to clad themselves in jet black waterproofs; they always seemed to be soaking wet summer and winter, and we always seemed to be in each other's way!

Of course, I worked with a lot of other fellows, and they were a great bunch and we had some super times together. Many of the older men I used to engage in discussions of their earlier days, and I revelled in tales of Claughtons, Precursors, Georges and lots of other LNWR types. As a connection with the past I recall one of the examining fitters, Andy Merrill, telling me how he used to shape the wooden brake blocks with an adze for some of the old LNWR tenders so as to fit the wheel circumference. After this they would take the blocks to the Blacksmith who would partly burn the edge of the block that went on to the wheel, to harden the timber. Stories of work during the war years were fascinating too, with the whole shed in darkness; indeed even in my day there was precious little lighting after dark. For working on the engines the only light we ever had were small paraffin flare lamps, which we used to fill up from the stores each morning and keep burning all day. The only exceptions were the Examining Fitters and Boilersmiths. The former had miners' type battery lamps that would attach to a belt around their waist, but unlike a miner they did not clip the lamp itself onto a helmet. These lamps were placed on charge in the stores when not in use. Boilersmiths, who spent most of their time in fireboxes, used acetylene carbide lamps, which gave a very bright light, and I often wondered why we were not similarly equipped.

The Brick Arch men were another breed on their own, who 'lived' in a small and rudimentary (this is the only word with which to describe it) wooden shack, cantilevered off the end of the fitters' cloak room. They spent most of their time in fireboxes, dismantling, repairing, or building new brick arches. This was an extremely dirty, dusty and to my mind awful job. If we had to go into the firebox for any reason we kept well away from the activities of these intrepid chaps! During my time a new type of brick arch was developed which was cast in place over a former, rather than built up of individual bricks – this seemed to make life just a little bit easier for these chaps and the resultant arches seemed to last longer. Other grades about the shed were the Steam Raisers, usually footplate men reduced in grade for some reason or other and 'Box Divers'. These unfortunates were labourers who descended into the fireboxes to clean all the accumulated remains of the combustion process. This was undertaken before the Boilersmiths started their examinations – it was to my mind an even worse job than that of the Brick Arch men. Incidentally, the usual reason for us to go into fireboxes was to repair the rocking grates, and to ensure that the various blow down pipes that discharged into the ash pan were correctly positioned – this was the only place one could see them easily. As well as this there were the Coalmen, who operated the coal and ash handling plants, the Tubers, who when not changing boiler tubes acted as Boilersmiths mates, Shunters, and many others. There were also several jobs that had dedicated staff, for example filling the sandboxes, and there was a Fitter's Mate on each shift who did nothing else but go around the shed filling the mechanical lubricators of engines; this was not a part of the drivers' preparation, they only had to check they were full.

As I said earlier I used to really enjoy working on engines in steam, the 'Y' scheme as it was called. The drill here was to collect from the Leading Fitter the repair cards given in by drivers as they brought engines to the shed. They were handed in to the Running Foreman and collected by the Leading Fitter. For this purpose the latter would make his way occasionally to the Running Foreman's office, which necessitated walking out of the Middle shed through the tunnel walkway (the aforementioned 'Gullet'). Now, at clocking off time we apprentices used to take turns in slipping away early, by clocking each other's cards. This was very handy for me so I did not have to run to catch the 5.5pm train home at the opposite end of the station. We had thus to be sure that the Leading Fitter had not gone to see the Running Foreman as we might bump into to him on his way back as we slipped up the tunnel – Tommy Brooks always seemed to have gone that way at clocking off

The unique 46205 PRINCESS VICTORIA on the North shed, about 1958. It had been converted so that the inside valve gear was driven via rockers from the outside gear – the other Princess Royals retained their original four separate sets of Walschaerts valve gear. Unlike the 'Big 'Uns' however, the rockers were ahead of the outside cylinders rather than behind – this was a less successful arrangement as it subjected the rocker movement, and thus the inside valves, to expansion of the outside valve rods. It had to be arranged thus due to the layout of the cylinders, with the outside ones situated over the trailing bogie wheels and therefore behind the inside ones. The engine is not long out of works and with a tender well full of coal; once the electrification works got under way it was no longer possible to pile tenders quite so high! The late George Wheeler was well known to the staff at Crewe North and often got the engines specially cleaned for his camera; this could well have been one of these occasions. (Late George Wheeler)

The 'Officers' Special' engine, Standard 2MT 2-6-0 78030, on what had been No.1 road of 'Abyssinia' shed on 11 April 1964. An extremely dilapidated scene by this time. (Dave Donkin)

time – and we were sure he did it on purpose. I have to say that personally I never got caught, but had some narrow scrapes! It is worth recording that when I first started work there was no time clock and this method of booking on and off was introduced later. We used to book on by collecting a brass 'check', a small circular plate about one and a half inches in diameter and stamped 'LNWR Loco Dept Crewe', with a number, 1875 in my case. We handed this in again when we booked off, and they were kept in a large wooden frame. This check was also used on pay day to collect our wages, given to us in a small tubular tin. We were supposed to open it and check the contents in the sight of the pay clerk and, after emptying, throw the tin in a large wicker basket set there for the purpose. This I was told had been the practice for at least the previous 65 years!

Reverting to the repair cards, after receiving them we would go to the engine arrangements board to see when the various engines were due off the shed, so that we could deal with them in order. We would then get whatever tools and material we needed, and make our way to the engine wherever it was. The board of course would have this information too. The sorts of jobs we did were piston rod packing, replacement water gauge glasses, brake adjustment and attending to faulty injectors not – losing water was the usual complaint in the case of exhaust injectors, or not changing over properly from live to exhaust steam, or vice versa. Steam and vacuum leaks were other common problems, along with knocks and bangs – one soon developed asbestos fingers! An examining fitter also carried out routine examination on engines working passenger and certain other trains and, on occasion, they would book repairs too, and we would deal with these. Often on this sort of work we would deal closely with the crews and some interesting situations might develop; the fitter would declare the engine fit to go and the driver insist it was not. For example, we could often get exhaust injectors to work without losing water by oiling the packing where the combining cone fitted into the injector body. But this rarely stood the test of time and as the oil dried out the water loss would start again. Of course most drivers knew of this trick, and would insist they had another engine and we would be left doing a more extensive repair ourselves, or stopping the engine for one of the 'X' scheme fitters to attend to it as they had more time. Sometimes we would have to get ourselves over to the station, to attend a driver's SOS whilst en route. The most frequent job would be a broken gauge glass, despite crews being trained to change them themselves. There were spare glasses and rubbers in the tool box but crews preferred to soldier on and then call on us.

I worked for some time with Albert Hickson, always known to everybody as 'Ab'. Ab had lost the sight of one eye in an accident with a hammer and chisel, where a piece of metal from the chisel head came adrift and lodged in his eye. This was of course a salutary lesson for a young apprentice as there was no eye protection available in those days – hence the need to always grind the chisel head so there was no possibility of bits flying off. Because of his eye, Ab always had an apprentice with him, and he only worked on the day shift. Among other things Ab did, and there were several, was acting as bookie's runner collecting bets from around the shed. He had a small metal case, somewhat akin to a lunch box and it had a timed lock so that once locked the time was recorded and only the bookmaker could open it. He would therefore accept the last bets before the first races and then close and lock the box taking it to the bookmaker on his way home. If he was on leave or away for any other reason, the apprentice with him at the time would assume this role, the box being brought in each morning by one of the other fitters who happened to pass Ab's house on his way to the shed! This was an interesting diversion, as one was expected to go all round the shed collecting bets, whilst when Ab did it himself, people came to him! Of course this was all very much outside the rules, but management turned a blind eye to it.

In those days too, I have to say Management turned a blind eye to other things, such as slipping out at lunchtime for a drink, despite the fact that we were paid right through with officially only a twenty minute paid meal break. On Fridays, pay-day, we used to go on a short pub-crawl having half a pint in each of several boozers.

We would start at the *Queens* in Station Street right outside the shed entrance and proceed thereafter in a sort of square. Next came the *Sterling Tap* and *The Locomotive*, both also in Station Street, followed after turning left into Mill Street by the *Lord Nelson, Albion* and *Express*. Another left turn would take us into Nantwich Road where we would call at the *Barrel* and then finish off in the *Royal*! After this we would make our way turning left again, along Pedley Street and a walkway at the back of the houses in Railway Street, and then via the Outdoor Machinery workshops 'creep' back into the shed, hopefully unseen! This would make four pints in all, but usually only the mild, which was very weak. Oh happy days!

Of course we did lots and lots of other jobs on locomotives – changing bearing springs was a common one. This could be a difficult task, especially if the threads on the spring bolts were rusty and seized – Ernie the Blacksmith would come in useful on such occasions with his oxy-acetylene torch to heat up the errant nuts. When underhung springs had to be changed the 'hurdy-gurdy' came into play. This was an 'A' frame piece of equipment that had a lifting chain passing over a drum where the cross piece was on the A; the chain, with a hook on the end of it, then passed over the sharp end of the frame on a pulley wheel. The whole contraption would be leant against the side of a locomotive and the chain could be shortened or lengthened by means of a handle on the drum; by these means springs could be hauled up from the pit bottom, or let down. One of us would operate the 'hurdy gurdy' whilst the other juggled about with the spring to get the bolt heads lined up with the holes in the spring top plate, and the axle box securing pin. I should add that this piece of kit had no mechanical advantage at all, so it was hard work to lift a spring up into position, and sometimes we would get a third hand to help.

Superheater elements were another lousy job, where you were stuck in a smoke box all day either removing or replacing the things. It was the joint from element to header that used to blow, and of course destroy the smoke box vacuum. When we got this job, first of all we would get the 'water bags', and standing at a distance hose out the smoke box with a high-pressure jet to remove as much of the muck and dirt as we could, but it was always a filthy job! When locomotives came on the shed for their 'X' day examinations, and before steam pressure dropped, an Examining Fitter would look for any steam blows or other repairs, test the injectors, brake equipment, steam heating apparatus and so on and 'book' any resulting repairs. If the driver had booked the engine as steaming badly, one of his jobs would be to apply steam against the brake and with the engine in mid-gear, open the smoke box door to see if any elements were leaking. All too often they seemed to find some!

Part of the No.8 V&P examination entailed removing the blast pipe to decarbonise it, and this was accomplished by mounting it an some arch bricks and lighting a large fire underneath. By these means the carbon was set alight and eventually burnt away. This was of course another job where apprentices would have great fun – almost setting the shed on fire on more than one occasion, and always getting the blast pipe glowing red hot! Another part of this examination was the removal of all the axle box underkeeps to clean out the oil reservoirs, examine the journals and renew or clean as necessary the 'Armstrong' oil pad. Some locomotives had roller bearing axle boxes and in these cases we would recharge them with new grease. The engine and tender would be split so that the intermediate draw gear could be examined and the drawbars renewed, or taken to the Blacksmith for tempering. For this job we had a massive 'G' clamp which took about three of us to manhandle. It was used to draw the engine and tender together against the pressure of the intermediate buffer springs, so we could get the securing pins in and out – the latter were always renewed by the way. And obviously at a V&P examination, as well as removing the valves and pistons for examination and fitting new rings, all the motion would come down. The rods and other parts would be taken to the machine shop where we would remove the bushes for remetalling and machining. The Turner would go to the engine and take the journal sizes by calliper, and then machine the bushes, after which we would cut and fit new oil pads, push the bushes back into the rods and then take the whole lot back to the engine ready for refitting. This was heavy work, especially on the three and four cylinder engines where we had to manhandle the inside motion, and in particular the connecting rods. For this reason the pits were very shallow – we would never have managed with the depth of pits in modern depots. The inside connecting rods of the Pacifics were all that two of us could handle, and it was a three man job to remove and replace them – the brasses too were almost as much as one man could lift alone.

I could of course go one for a lot longer, but I think and hope I have not only illustrated something of what I got up to in the early days but also something of the North Shed, and how locomotives were maintained. It was a most absorbing time for me, and the enormous impression it had on me has I hope, come out in this description – I can remember it all so clearly it seems like only yesterday. It gives me enormous pleasure and satisfaction that I was able to work on steam locomotives when they were going about their normal business. I was only just in time, as during the course of my apprenticeship they were almost eliminated from everyday use in this country. To see how they were allowed to fall into such awful condition very shortly after I moved on to diesels for a spell was quite disheartening. That I was able to do this at the No.1 passenger locomotive depot on the London Midland Region was a bonus, and I shall ever be grateful to Geoff Sands, unfortunately no longer with us, for giving me this start to an absorbing and enjoyable railway career, of over 40 subsequent years.

Britannia 70050 FIRTH OF CLYDE in the yard at Crewe North during the summer of 1964. A number – at one time twenty or so – were allocated to Crewe, generally in the period 1962-65, to replace Royal Scots as they were withdrawn. This is one of the Britannias with the larger coal capacity high-sided tenders, originally allocated to the Scottish Region. 'Middle' shed behind with one of the Ivatt 2-6-2Ts outside. (JB Bucknall)

Some indications of early developments at Crewe

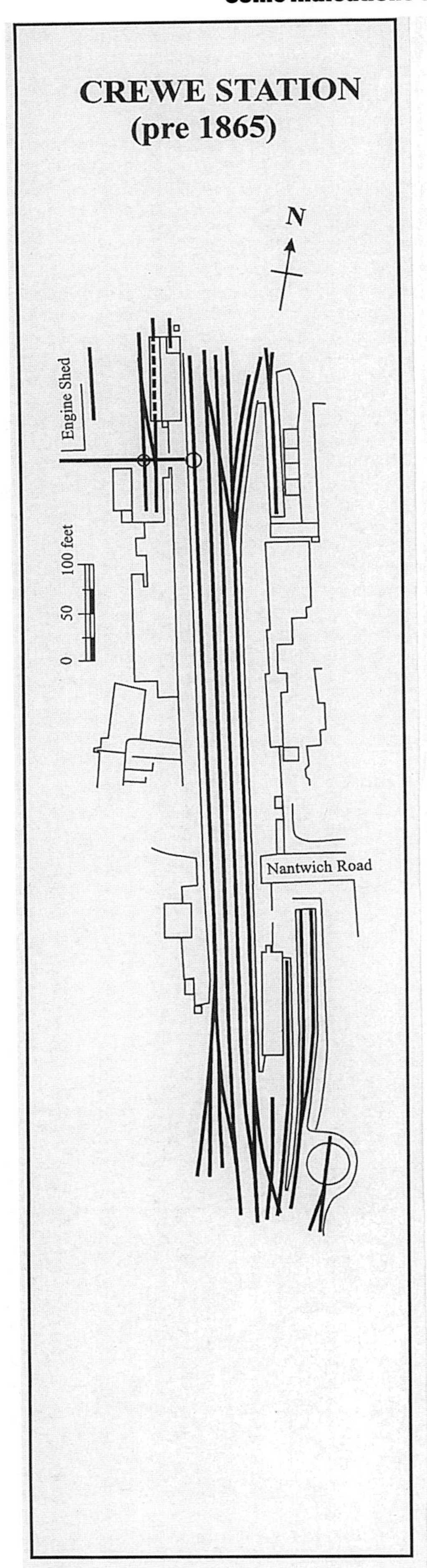

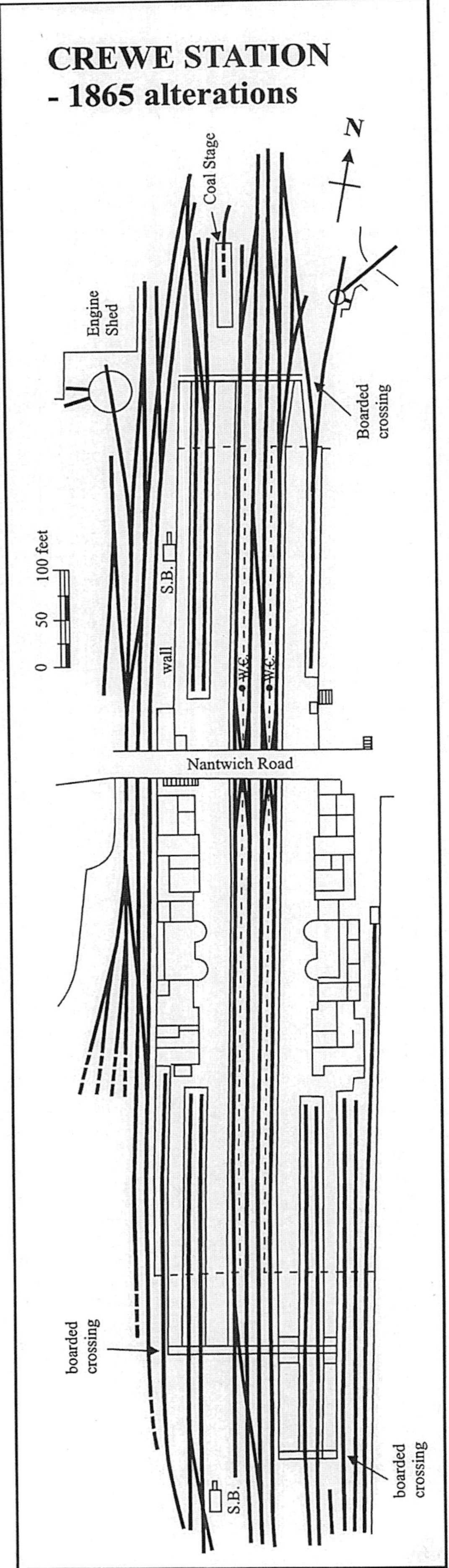

Interval 1: Crewe Generalities

Crewe North Junction just prior to the last war, with 'Baby Scot' 5518, then unnamed, entering the station with a train from the north. Beneath is a train is just leaving the station for the North Wales Coast with a Class 5 in charge. The large building in the centre is part of the Works Oil and Grease plant, with the line to Manchester curving away to its right; on the extreme right are the Up Hill Carriage Sidings. (RS Carpenter)

When they were built the last two Stanier Pacifics, as modified by Ivatt, had an altered rear end and trailing truck and were later fitted with electric lighting. Here is 46257 CITY of SALFORD on the Vacuum Pits in Crewe Works, and both the electric lighting and modified rear end can be clearly seen. Notice the steam turbo generator just behind the smoke deflectors. It would appear that at this particular works visit the engine had been fitted with AWS equipment – note the freshly painted protection plate for the receiver under the draw hook. The occasion is in all probability a Unclassified Repair, recorded on the engine record cards as having taken place between 7 January and 8 February 1960. Further confirmation of the date comes from the Royal Scot seen alongside, 46121 HIGHLAND LIGHT INFANTRY, CITY of GLASGOW REGIMENT, which was also recorded in the works for part of this period, in its case between 18 December 1959 and 2 February 1960. The electric lighting equipment was later removed from 46247 and sister locomotive 46256. In this picture, doubtless taken during a Sunday enthusiast visit, the engines would be waiting steam testing the following day before return to traffic – that is what happened on the Vacuum Pits. The Pacific needs a front coupling. (DH Beecroft, The Transport Treasury)

Two pre-war views of Platform 5 at Crewe station, the first looking north (note the bridge taking the Nantwich Road over the railway) and the second looking south. Both reveal the rather woebegone state of the place at this time. The clock has moved around five minutes between the photographer taking the two shots.

Looking north along No.1 Platform (on the left) on 4 October 1956. Just arrived is the Western Region through train from Bristol; the nearest vehicle, at least, will terminate here. It could be the 8.38am ex-Bristol which carried through coaches to Manchester and Chester – this train (as would be expected, it is made up of WR coaches) was due in Crewe at 12.37. Note the ex-LNER bogie brake in No.7 Bay – this was later renumbered 1A. Actually, all the bay platforms at Crewe were renumbered in about 1958, with an 'A' suffix for those at the north end and a 'B' suffix for those at the south end.

Patricroft Jubilee 45559 BRITISH COLUMBIA at the side of the Paint Shop on 28 March 1954. Old Mr Irwell's 'The Book of The Jubilee 4-6-0s', tells us that between 1 March and 1 April 1954 45559 was in Crewe Works for a heavy intermediate repair, and that it was back for 'Rectification' within six days of leaving. Oh dear, I wonder what the problem was? It certainly needs a front coupling! (AW Battson, The Transport Treasury)

Outside the Paint Shop in June 1958 with Princess Royal 46210 LADY PATRICIA, an Edge Hill resident at the time. Between 13 April and 7 June 1958 it is recorded as in Crewe Works for 'Rectification' following a Heavy General Repair – its last – in February-March the same year. One is left wondering why whatever it was that was wrong took so long to fix, and why the engine is standing here. (DH Beecroft, The Transport Treasury)

Crewe North Junction looking north on 1 July 1950, and a Class 5 hauled train departs for the north from No.1 Platform. From left to right we can see: the extreme north end of the 'Middle' shed at Crewe North, the Old Works buildings, the North Junction signal box just above the engine, the main line north and, to its right, the Works Oil and Grease Plant. The line to Manchester curves away to the extreme right. The Class 4 2-6-4T shunting in the Up Hill Sidings would be the 'Bank Engine' (the colloquial term for the engine allocated to the Up Hill Siding Shunt) on this day. Notice the train spotters on the island platform 3 and 4 – a few years later I would be one of their number! (MN Bland, Transport Treasury)

Crewe South shed, and what looks like a brand new 9F, 92223 having recently arrived off the works and awaiting lighting up and despatch. This engine was from the last batch built at Crewe, recorded as new on 6 June 1958; its first allocation was Banbury. The 9F behind, 92043, was one of the first batch built at Crewe and completed in January 1955. This one was allocated to Annesley at this period and would not, therefore, normally find its way to Crewe, so had doubtless paid a visit to 'The Works'. (DH Beecroft, The Transport Treasury)

The Up 'Royal Scot' passing through No.4 through road on 28 March 1954. This was a period when Camden Pacifics were diagrammed to work through from Carlisle to Euston, with the crew on a 'double home' diagram. The engine is 46244 KING GEORGE V with the later 'diesel style' headboard. Note there is no coal visible in the tender! At this time the train only made one intermediate stop, at Carlisle, where it was due to depart at 11.57am having changed the Polmadie Pacific for the Camden one. It was due in Euston at 5.30pm. The time would be about 3 o' clock, assuming the train was running to time. Notice the fireman taking a breather – only another 158 miles to go – and the lovely old van used by the Civil Engineer in the spur road. Trains that did not stop at Crewe were never common, and even at the time this picture was taken the Down 'Royal Scot' called there. (AW Battson, The Transport Treasury)

Four unusual views follow of Crewe town itself on 19 May 1955, the eve of demolition of a large part of the housing in the area now occupied by the inevitable shopping centre. These were all of course, 'railway houses', built by the LNWR for its workers. This first one is Market Terrace looking west. It lay immediately north of the Market Square. As these houses were for the managers, they are three stories and have porches! As can be seen, demolition is already underway; notice the Potteries Demolition sign on the left-hand house. The monument is the Crewe Town War Memorial which as one would expect has engraved on it the names of many railwaymen, along with others from the town, who gave their lives in the two World Wars.

Right. View looking along Market Terrace due north towards Victoria Street; notice that the road is part closed for the demolition work.

Left. This is Sandbach Street, looking north towards Victoria Street. As these house were for lesser mortals, they have neither a third story nor porches. Demolition is not under way yet, and the houses are still occupied.

Right. Charles Street, looking north towards Victoria Street – all the streets in these views ran parallel to each other between Delemere Street and Victoria Street. The houses all dated from the middle of the 19th Century and these particular ones, still only two storeys but with a porch and thus mid-way between worker and manager in style and extent were, naturally, for foremen! Crewe was of course, the first railway town, and not only did the railway company provide houses, but water and gas supplies too, from its own works of course.

Liverpool portion of the 9.5am Birmingham to Liverpool and Manchester train leaving Crewe on Good Friday 4 April 1958. Class 5 45043 is, unusually for this working, a Mold Junction engine. Crewe North shed is to the left. (Michael Mensing)

The south end of Crewe Station, with Edge Hill Royal Scot 46158 THE LOYAL REGIMENT departing from platform 4 on 28 March 1954. With a fully coaled tender it must have come on the train at Crewe. I would wager that the train is the 12.45 Bangor-Euston, due out of Crewe at 3.24pm. A nice clean exhaust, a whisper from the safety valves and a slight blow from the piston rod packing, combine to make this a very pleasing early spring scene. (AW Battson, The Transport Treasury)

The south end of the station on 28 March 1954, with Camden's 46146 THE RIFLE BRIGADE on a train at No.3 platform. The Scot would have come on at Crewe judging by the amount of coal in the tender. The train could well be the combined Windermere and Blackpool to London, due away from Crewe at 2.18pm, for a non-stop run due Euston at 5.3pm. I opt for this train in view of the leading coach, as it was usual at the time to use older vehicles like this on the less prestigious trains. One of the early Caprotti valve gear fitted Class 5s can just be discerned to the right. (AW Battson, The Transport Treasury)

The Chester bays, as they were known, at the north end of the station on 26 November 1960. On the left in bay 2A is 45571 SOUTH AFRICA (a Blackpool engine at the time) with the 12.15pm to Blackpool and on the right with the 12.8pm to Bangor is EE Type 4 D216, in the days before the yellow front end warning panels. Another Jubilee awaits its next job on the extreme left. (Michael Mensing)

Royal Scot 46162 QUEEN'S WESTMINSTER RIFLEMAN, a Carlisle Kingmoor engine, standing on No.2 through road at the north end of Crewe in the 1950s. The engine would have arrived with a train from the north – no coal visible in the tender – and is waiting for the signal to proceed to the North shed. (DH Beecroft, The Transport Treasury)

The north end of Platform 2 on Good Friday, 31 March 1961, with EE Type 4 D306 on the 1.5pm Euston to Holyhead. No yellow warning panel yet and the ladder still in place on the nose end – these were soon removed for obvious reasons once the overhead wires for the electrification started to be erected. As a Sunday service was provided on this day, the train was due away from Crewe at 5.35pm and due Holyhead at 9.11pm; over eight hours from London to Holyhead! Beyond is the famous 'Coffee Tavern', well known to all engine crews as it was open 24 hours a day. Although it was never advertised as such, it was available to the general public too, and I recall hours spent there after evening classes at the technical school, if I had missed the train home! (Michael Mensing)

The south end of Crewe Station on 14 September 1961, with 46231 DUCHESS of ATHOLL on No.4 through road, waiting the arrival of the afternoon Manchester and Liverpool to West of England trains. After combining them and adding this extra coach, it was due away from Crewe at 1.13pm. This is a fill-in turn, the Polmadie Duchess having arrived at Crewe with an overnight train from Glasgow. It would only work the Plymouth train as far a Shrewsbury, where a Shrewsbury Castle would take over. The Duchess would then turn on the Severn Bridge Triangle, before working the return service back to Crewe due to leave Shrewsbury at 3.49pm, arrival at 4.36pm. It would then be facing the right way to return to Glasgow on an overnight train the same evening. These types of 'fill-in' turns were regular diagrams at Crewe for both Polmadie and Crewe North Pacifics and between their nightly excursions to and from Scotland. However, by this date it was getting less common, as the Type 4 diesels had started to make their inroads! (A Roscoe, The Transport Treasury)

For a few years the Derby inspired and built first ten Peaks (later Class 44) were allocated to the Western Lines of the LMR, and here is one of them. The train is the 12.50pm Barrow and Blackpool (combined at Preston) to Euston, due away from Crewe at 2.44 on this Sunday, 5 March 1961. D5 CROSS FELL, allocated to Camden at the time, is at the south end of Platform 4. Later all ten went to the Midland Lines. (Michael Mensing)

Princess Royal Pacific 46203 PRINCESS MARGARET ROSE, waiting to depart from No.4 platform with a Liverpool-London train some time in March 1960. Edge Hill had these engines for many years, indeed until they were all withdrawn, and they were of course, regular performers on its London turns. Notice that by this date the engine has AWS equipment – observe the protection plate behind the front coupling – and a speedometer, driven from the trailing crank. Despite the overhead electrification wires being in place and energised by this date, no staff warning 'flashes' are fixed to the locomotive. (DH Beecroft, The Transport Treasury)

The 'Salop Bays', Nos.3A and 4A at the south end of the station on 23 September 1961, with the 5.20pm to Wellington waiting to depart. This train would run via the Western Region branch from Nantwich through Market Drayton to join the Shrewsbury-Wolverhampton route just west of Wellington. The engine is Wellington - based Ivatt Class 2 2-6-2T 41232, a long-term resident of that shed and a regular on these Crewe workings. The two coach formation was quite normal at the time, the Ivatts having replaced Western Region pannier tanks used in earlier times. The engine is bunker first, although it was more normal to turn them on one or other of the triangles at Gresty Lane, or even on the turntable on the South shed. For servicing however, engines working the branch via Market Drayton used the former GWR shed at Gresty Lane, and not the North or South sheds. This continued until the branch passenger service ceased on 9 September 1963. It remained open for a number of years for freight and to act as a diversionary route – at one time it was even used by the 'Pines Express'. The building on the left is the former GWR Booking Office, the Great Western having its own facilities at Crewe in pre-nationalisation days, and the platform to the left of this is No.3, in those times the only one available for bi-directional working. (Michael Mensing)

The south end of the station, about 1962 I would say, showing 46250 CITY OF LICHFIELD of Carlisle Upperby, heading back along No.2 through road and destined for the North shed. The engine would have arrived from the north earlier – notice no coal visible in tender – perhaps having brought in the train seen on the left in No.3 platform. The English Electric Type 4 diesel just behind the tender is at the head of a train in No.3 platform, and an electric locomotive can just be discerned in the distance. (The Transport Treasury)

Maroon painted Duchess 46228 DUCHESS of RUTLAND of Crewe North, waiting at the south end of No.4 through road with extra vehicles to attach to an Up train due to arrive at either No.4 or No.5 platforms. When the train arrives and its engine has been detached, the Duchess will attach the extra vehicles and work the train south. Although undated I would place this picture as 1961. Notice the engine carries a Class 2 passenger train headlamp code, so perhaps the train it was to work forward was a Class 2, but what that would be I cannot say – it might it be just be a 'lazy' fireman not having set the code correctly. (The Transport Treasury)

The new Nantwich Road station entrance, shortly after completion in late 1960 – it remains substantially unaltered to this day, though of course there is much more road traffic. Crossville was the local bus operator and one of the familiar Bristol Loadeka double Decker buses is in evidence. View looks east towards Sandbach. (British Railways)

A modern view of the Independent lines, as they descend into the tunnel taking them under Crewe North Junction. Here we see Class 87 electric locomotive 87027, during the period of the extensive remodelling of the layout when the station itself was completely closed. Hence normal passenger services used these lines; the train in this case is the 10.20 Euston to Liverpool, on 8 June 1985. On the left are the Chester Independent lines, descending from the North Junction to a junction with the other routes at Salop Goods Junction, the signal box there just being visible through the left-hand bridge span – the bridge carries the Nantwich Road over the railway, and the view is looking south. The left-hand lines in the foreground are the Manchester Independents, and those on the right the Liverpool Independents. Notice the train conveys a Mark One catering vehicle. (Colin Boocock)

CREWE DIESEL DEPOT - 1968

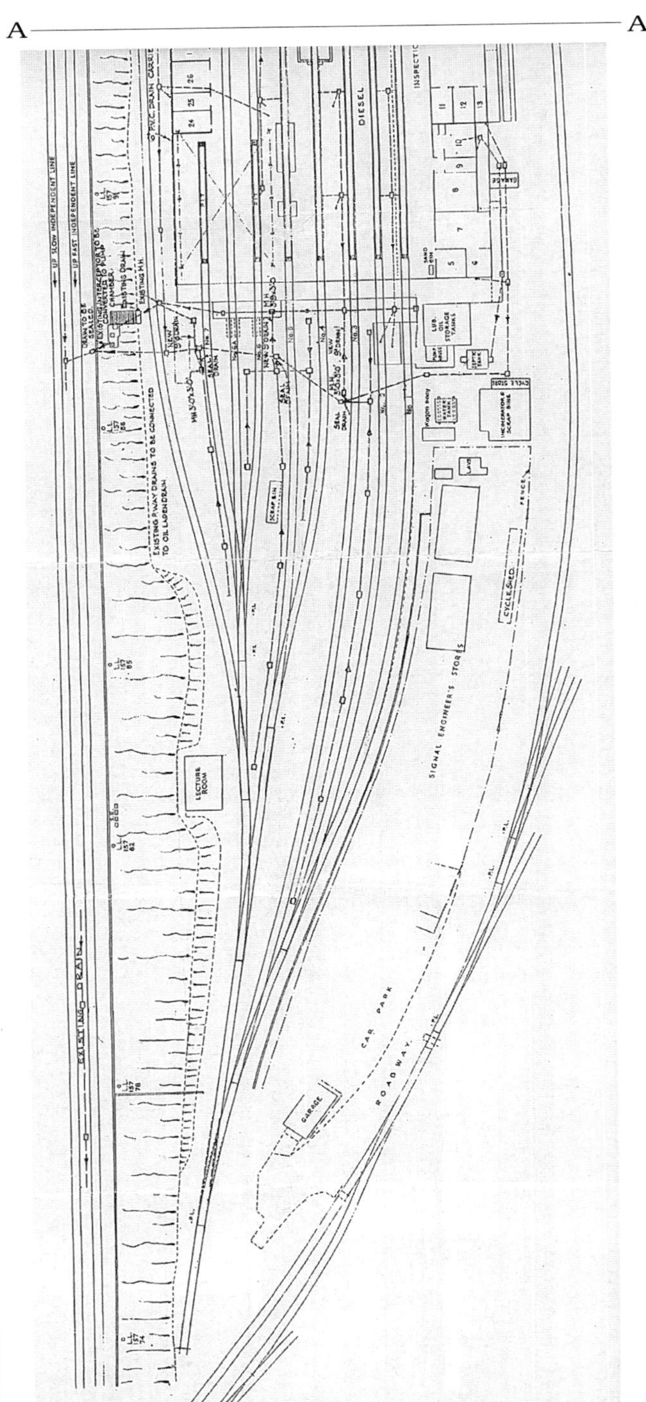

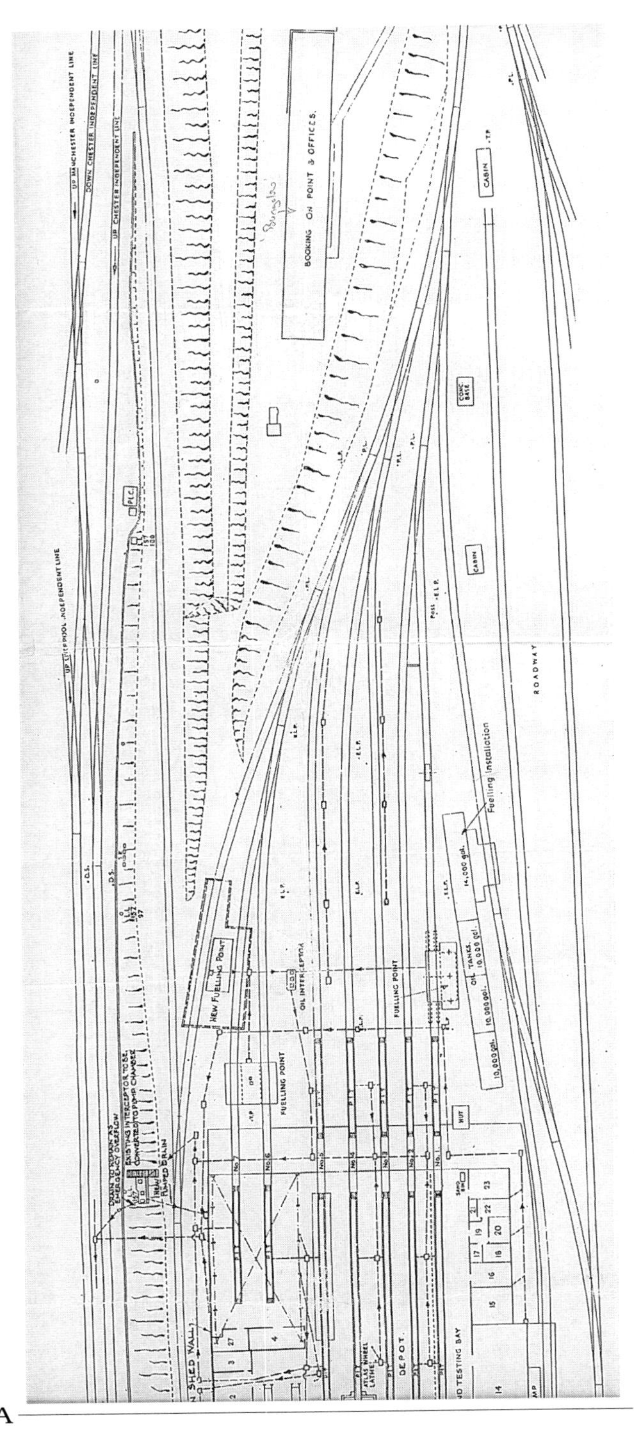

ARRANGEMENT OF OFFICE. WORKSHOP. AND STORE ACCOMMODATION.

1. Store for Boiler descaling acid
2. Space for Drill and Grindstone
3. Compressor Room
4. Sub Station
5. Lecture Room
6. Kitchen
7. Mess Room
8. Locker Room
9. Ambulance Room
10. Male Lavatory
11. Tool Store
12. Lock-up Store
13. Stores Office
14. Store
15. Boiler House
16. Fuel Store
17. Depot Supervisor's Office
18. Depot Foreman and Assistant's Office
19. Fitters' Lobby
20. Shift Mechanical/Electrical Foreman. Shop Officeman and Work Study Assessor's Office
21. Book Room
22. Clerk and R.S.I. Office
23. Filter Cleaning Room
24. Injector Testing Room
25. Battery Room
26. Space for Fitters' Lockers
27. Room for storing Work Study Documents

Chapter Two
Examination and Repair Depot

The history of locomotive maintenance and operating practices on the main line railways of this country is both diverse and fascinating, with each of the old pre-grouping companies adopting its own individual approach. After the 1923 Grouping of the former companies into the 'Big Four', as the new companies were called, the new masters gradually brought some form of consistency into their respective methods. Then, after Nationalisation, the new Railway Executive did likewise, but with ex-LMS men dominating the top echelons of the Motive Power, Operating and Chief Mechanical Engineer's Departments, it was no surprise to see the practices of the erstwhile LMS being gradually promulgated through the entire system. One significant LMS idea was that of concentrating the heavier shed examinations and repairs at a relatively few depots, and this perhaps was to manifest itself to the ultimate in the post-war plans for Crewe.

Interior of the new 'Examination and Repair Depot', more familiar in later years as simply the 'Diesel Depot', on 27 September 1955 prior to completion. These are the three southern bays with the workshop area beyond. Behind the wall was the electricity sub-station.

It is true of course, that the other railways had also concentrated some of their heavier examinations and repairs, but this tended to be dictated by the facilities the depots already had, whilst the LMS went about specifically equipping depots, and moving equipment about to meet their aim. (Such sheds were usually those with an 'A' suffix to their codes.) The LMS therefore, had by far the most thoroughly worked out system, and Colonel Rudgard, who had championed it as the Motive Power Officer, brooked no deviations. As Harold Rudgard took the top Motive Power post in the nationalised system, it was a foregone conclusion that LMS practice would prevail. The GWR I am told had something quite close to the LMS way of doing things, but the LNER was by all accounts not a little lax – as one of my former colleagues put it: 'Why pull up daisies to check the roots?'

At the close of the Second World War locomotive servicing and maintenance at Crewe North Shed was in many respects literally on its last legs. Crewe boasted two principal sheds; North to the north of the station and South, situated south of the station. Between them they housed not only one of the largest concentrations of locomotives on the former LMS system, by this time part of the London Midland Region, but on the entire British railway system. Their history is both long and interesting, and has been well covered elsewhere; suffice to say here, that the North Shed site dated from about 1848, and the South Shed 1896. The latter came about for several reasons. First the need for additional locomotive facilities as traffic grew and secondly remodelling of the station to handle the increased traffic, which required the demolition of one of the buildings at the North Shed. Thirdly, there was a requirement to reduce the number of light engine movements between the developing marshalling yards at Basford Hall, south of Crewe station, and the sheds north of the station. Thus came about the practice, which persisted until the North Shed closed in October 1965, of housing the passenger engines at the North Shed and goods and mineral engines at the South Shed.

The stores loading dock looking north, 11 March 1958. This is the east side of the shed; beyond it can be seen the windows of the office block.

The messing, locker and other domestic facilities adjacent to the stores and its loading dock, 11 March 1958. To the right is the Down Yard and the roadway to the South shed.

Crewe as a location to operate, maintain and repair locomotives was of course ideal, lying as it does at the centre of the old LNWR system and being such an important junction. From Crewe the lines radiate to London, Shrewsbury along with Wales and the South West, the North Wales Coast, Liverpool and the north, Manchester, Stoke-on-Trent and Derby. As a point where passengers changed trains its credentials are legendary, and few 'regular' rail travellers cannot have had at least one experience of its apparently mysterious working practices. Thus it became one of the principal locomotive centres in Britain, the two sheds having for many years a combined allocation of something in the region of 400 locomotives.

The North Shed always had a large allocation of whatever the principal express passenger engines were at any one time. These of course included the early LNWR types, culminating in the George the Fifth and Precursor 4-4-0s and the Prince of Wales and Claughton 4-6-0s. These were followed by the LMS Compounds and then the Royal Scots. The Scots in turn were supplemented/supplanted by the Princess Royal and Coronation Pacifics, Jubilee 4-6-0s and later, in BR days, Britannia Pacifics.

The LMS was in the forefront of the 'Big Four' in its efforts to improve the efficiency and productivity of its operations, particularly during the 1930s when the Depression began to really hurt. The various cost-saving drives under the leadership of Sir Josiah Stamp have passed into legend. As President of the Executive – a new post – he had been appointed in January 1926, abolishing in the process the time-honoured position of General Manager.

Coming from an economic, rather than a railway or even transport background, Stamp's appointment was unprecedented in its day and his experience of the North American way of doing things soon brought other senior people into the Company from similar backgrounds. A particular appointment to illustrate this was that of Sir Harold Hartley, an Oxford Don and PhD, and again with no railway experience hitherto, and a Scientist to boot. Hartley became 'Vice President Works and Ancillary Undertakings' as well as Director of Research – this included operating research as well as its more conventional connotations. These and other moves were unprecedented in the industry, and from them developed a massive programme of improvements in the efficiency and productivity of everything the railway did.

One of the principal initiatives was the drive to improve locomotive utilisation, and this embraced every facet of their maintenance, both in the sheds and at main workshops, including repairs, servicing and day-to-day operation, including manning, diagramming and so on. The resulting improvement in miles run per engine, and reduction in the miles per casualty are legendary, and need not detain us here, except one particular facet. There was clearly a need to get the utmost levels of utilisation from the expensive express passenger Pacifics the Company was building in the 1930s. The trick was to build just enough Pacifics for those trains which could be run most economically with such expensive engines; the better the locomotives could be matched to the services, the better for all concerned. From this came the decision to concentrate all the No.8 Valve and Piston (V&P) shed maintenance examinations on the entire fleet of these locomotives at Crewe North, no matter what shed they were allocated to. This practice started about 1938 when the two classes were allocated to Camden, Edge Hill, Polmadie and Crewe North itself and continued, with the exception of those Pacifics that found themselves in the Scottish Region at Nationalisation, until the engines were withdrawn from service. The No.8 V&P was the largest of the scheduled examinations undertaken at the sheds, as opposed to main workshops.

There were a number of reasons why this could be expected to improve the performance of these locomotives and, equally importantly, their utilisation. In the first instance it proved possible to have dedicated teams of men working on a two shift system of days and nights, and the experience and knowledge thus gained, both reduced the time taken for the work and ensured a consistency of standards. Secondly, the close proximity of North Shed to Crewe Works – the maintaining works for the classes –

The complete shed on 17 September 1955, looking east from the Independent lines – Salop Goods Junction signal box is just off the picture to the left.

The north bays, with overhead crane and raised platform, specially adapted for the maintenance of diesel shunting locomotives. The date is November 1957, and Fitters Fred Bayman to the right and Harry Brownridge to the left are lowering down a cylinder head they have removed from the locomotive. On the left can be seen Fitter Bob Capewell working at a bench. Fred Bayman later became a Leading Fitter and then a Shift Foreman, while Bob, after spells at Carnforth and Barrow, became Depot Foreman. Notice to the right one of the ex-LMS jackshaft drive diesel-electric shunters.

made it possible to easily transfer any parts needing 'Works' attention that were beyond the capabilities of the shed, both quickly and cheaply. For example, it was LMS and later LMR practice not to let the sheds repair piston valves, save for cleaning and ring renewal and, as the engines had needle roller bearings in some of their motion joints – notably the combination lever and union link – these parts had to go to the 'Works' if they needed attention too. Moreover, it was often possible to keep locomotives out of 'Works' for longer periods by specific attention to various other parts that otherwise needed such attention. Often this could be given by teams of 'Works' staff coming across to the shed, together with any specialist items of equipment and doing the job there.

The whole arrangement worked extremely well and once the entire fleet was in service two locomotives would be 'stopped' at any one time with each one taking five days, or ten shifts from start to finish for the examination and any repairs arising. This practice continued during the war years when it became even more important to maintain and improve locomotive utilisation and, as I have said, until the final demise of the engines concerned. In BR days national feelings came into it and, as already mentioned, the Scottish Region insisted on doing the work themselves, at Polmadie. Crewe remained the maintaining Works but the policy resulted in lower utilisation, and lower mileages accrued to the Scottish engines compared to their contemporaries south of the border.

At the risk of repeating a few points (these chapters are designed to be self-standing, separate essays after all) it might be worthwhile here to briefly describe the examination sequence for steam locomotives, whereby engines employed on express passenger and some mixed traffic duties were stopped weekly for what was known as an 'X' day examination. Lesser types had their 'X' days at 14 day intervals. This examination was quite general, and included any repairs booked by drivers and deferred until the engine was out of steam, and any work located after a thorough examination by an Examining Fitter with the engine both in steam and cold. At the same time if a boiler washout was due this would be undertaken too, the periodicity of wash outs largely depending on the quality of water being used, some engines being washed out at seven day intervals, and others 14 day intervals – thus the terms BFX, and WOX, indicating Boiler Full X, or Washout X. As well as the 'X' examination, moving parts were maintained on a mileage basis, and static ones on a time basis, the latter generally on a 3-5 week or 7-9 week periodicity, and with any mileage examinations due all the work would be concentrated with the 'X' day work, often of course taking far longer than a single day to complete. There were of course exceptions to these brief guidelines, for example locomotives engaged on shunting and trip work would only have mileage examinations – this work covering the valves, pistons and motion – as and when 'booked', that is blowing and or knocking!

Returning now to the state of Crewe North after the War, by this time the northlight pattern 'Webb' style Stock Shed, dating from 1891-92, the westernmost of the three sheds then standing, was in a very woebegone state, and almost devoid of any roof. This was surprising, as for years it had not been used for engines in steam but, rather as its name infers, for storing engines not in use. As well as this, both the Middle Shed of 1865 and 'Abba' of 1868 were also well past their prime. As described in the previous chapter, far-reaching LMS plans to comprehensively remodel Crewe North did not come to full fruition, or anything like it, though modernisation work commenced in 1948, the first year of Nationalisation.

To enable the work to go ahead whilst the depot continued to function, a lot of the heavier repairs and mileage examination work was transferred away, but not the Pacifics I hasten to add. Instead some of the Class 6 and 7 engines, the Royal Scots and 5XPs, were dealt with at Manchester Longsight. For the extra work some of the young Crewe North fitters were temporarily transferred too, for example Geoff Oliver and Cliff Walker. In the remodelling at Crewe North (to repeat

Inside the new shed in November 1957. The view is northwards with the roads numbered 1-5 from right (west) to left (east). The workshop is to the left; on the right were all the other rooms and offices.

somewhat from Chapter One) the intention was to completely replace the existing three sheds, with two full roundhouses, each roundhouse having completely independent coal and ash handling plants, in fact almost two independent sheds side by side. The concept was that each set of facilities would function separately from the other, so as to keep the depot fully working during any subsequent repairs or maintenance. As a prelude to all this the Stock Shed and much of 'Abba' were demolished and a section of the new No.2 roundhouse, along with its coal and ash handling plants were completed. Meantime, the Middle Shed was left to soldier on almost alone, housing all engines in need of maintenance and repair. For reasons we shall see later, this was as far as the work progressed at the North Shed.

Another part of the scheme was the complete separation of the heavier maintenance and repairs, indeed almost any attention apart from boiler washing where the locomotive need not be in steam. It had long been realised that the heavier shed repair work was never going to be fully successful where locomotives in steam were also present, with all their attendant daily needs. It was the plan at Crewe, therefore, to build a new shed completely separate from the existing site and specially equipped to undertake mileage examinations and heavy repairs, including removal of wheels. There would be adequate equipment and machinery for this level of work for the entire passenger and mixed traffic locomotive fleet allocated to the Western Lines sheds of the LMR. To this end a spacious 280ft long double ended depot was to be built, 141ft wide with five through roads and five 80ft bay roads, three at one end and two at the other.

The site chosen was south of the station on the west side between the 'Old Yard' and the Independent lines. It was occupied by a very large mound of earth and clay, excavated and placed there in the period 1896-1901 when the cuttings and tunnels were built, as referred to earlier. This scheme embraced the Independent lines, the station enlargements and the South Shed. Known as the 'Big Dig', over 1,000 men had been employed at a cost of some £500,000. A series of lines were built which bypassed the station area, hence the term Independent lines, from south of the Basford Hall marshalling yards to north of the station. There was a deep cutting through which the lines passed, west of where the new depot was to be constructed. Moving this mound of earth took some time, and most of it went by rail to the railway-owned tip at Betley, five miles south of Crewe.

The new establishment was to be known as the 'Examination and Repair Depot' and the equipment and facilities were nothing short of a revelation in steam locomotive maintenance terms. It was a fully heated, light and airy building with fluorescently lit inspection pits, excellent messing arrangements and wash rooms that included showers – absolutely unheard of hitherto. The mess facilities were sufficient for 100 staff, with 80 on duly at any one time. The two bay roads at the north end were specially equipped with sole bar height platforms and a 2-½ ton electric overhead travelling crane, for the maintenance of the diesel shunting locomotives allocated to Crewe South, but otherwise the whole building was for the 'Concentration' repairs of steam locomotives. The area between the bays on the west side of the building housed the workshop area, and as well as the Machine Shop there were separate workshops for the Blacksmith, Coppersmith and White Metaller. The Machine Shop was well equipped with a 12in gap lathe, radial arm drilling machine, 12in shaper, 9½in centre lathe and smooth and rough grinders. In addition, No.5 road was to have at its centre point a 'Standard' electric wheel drop and there was to be an axle journal turning lathe. All these items first appeared on drawings labelled 'Examination & Repair Shop', in June 1954; construction commenced in mid-1955, the main contractor being Leonard Fairclough Limited of Adlington in Lancashire.

As events turned out it became increasingly apparent as construction progressed over the next 18 months, that the future of motive power on Britain's railways did not lie with steam. The decision was therefore made to use the new depot for the maintenance of diesel locomotives rather than steam, with Crewe North and South forced to soldier on and see out steam traction. The decision seems to have been made in early 1957, and drawings dated June the following year are titled: 'Alterations for Diesels'. Most of the machine tools, which would of course have been of little use for diesel maintenance, were already installed but it was possible to cancel the axle journal lathe and the wheel drop. The latter was replaced by an 'Atlas' underfloor wheel reprofiling machine which conveniently utilised the large hole already dug for the drop pit. This machine was capable of re-profiling wheel sets while still in position in the locomotive, for it was calculated that the smaller wheels and anticipated higher annual mileages for the new traction would require such attention much more frequently than their steam counterparts. This prediction turned out to be completely correct and such machines became invaluable in keeping locomotives out of main workshops for long periods, and indeed still do. On the debit side, it should be mentioned that wheel sets on modern traction are also more susceptible to tread and flange damage. This is particularly so where disc brakes are used and also on powered wheels. Often, complete vehicle wheel sets have to be re-profiled at the same time.

Other items added at this time included a 2½ ton electric overhead travelling crane over the bay roads at the south end. It was similar to the one over the north end bays but had powered longitudinal movement. The one at the other end of the shed was moved by hand. There was also a diesel fuelling installation with 14,000 gallon storage tanks, along with injector servicing and oil testing facilities. To the east of the main building the offices, stores and amenity block ran the whole length of the shed, 27ft wide increasing to 33ft for the area of the stores. Rail access was from the northern end, with all eight shed roads converging into a single neck at the south end. There was a run-round at the west side. Additionally there was an emergency connection between No.1 shed road and the Old Yard, the shed roads being numbered from the east, Old Yard side. While the new depot was certainly an improvement on the average steam shed, it lacked much in the sort of staff amenities that were soon to become very much the norm in later, purpose-built depots. For example there was no car park, and the offices, mess room and toilets were rather Spartan.

From 16 September 1957, with the introduction of the winter timetable the Stoke to Derby train service went over to diesel multiple unit (DMU) operation, and initially facilities were provided to service the sets at Crewe Carriage Shed. This was south of the station on the up, opposite side of the main lines to the South shed; it was in the apex between the main line south and the North Stafford line to Stoke. Whilst the servicing and minor repairs to the new units were undertaken there, anything bigger, once a Crewe allocation of the new units was established, necessitated the sets going to the new 'Examination and Repair Depot', which seems to have become operational in the early months of 1958. However, as the roads within the new depot had conventional pits, they were by no means ideal for DMUs with their underslung engines and transmissions. When the numbers of main line diesel locomotives started to increase with the delivery of the EE Type 4s, opportunity was taken to transfer the sets to the purpose-built DMU depot that had meantime been constructed at Stoke-on-Trent, at Cockshute Sidings. However, the DMUs continued to be serviced and receive minor repairs at the carriage shed, where one of the pits had been specially deepened for the purpose.

Once established for the maintenance of diesel main line locomotives Crewe Diesel Depot, as it became known, started to undertake the larger examinations and repairs on the entire fleet of English Electric Type 4 locomotives allocated to the LMR Western Lines sheds. As well as Crewe North, these were Camden, Manchester Longsight, Liverpool Edge Hill and Carlisle. As the numbers of these locomotives increased more and more of the younger fitters were transferred to the Diesel Depot from the North and South sheds, and the annual intake of apprentices were stepped up.

Servicing, together the smaller 'A' examinations and running repairs to the diesels were not, however, carried out at the new depot, rather it continued to be the preserve of the two steam sheds with their somewhat crude facilities. The South shed installation dated from before the war when diesel shunting locomotives were introduced in the Basford Hall marshalling yards. Rudimentary facilities had been

The three southern bays in November 1957, before a 2½ ton overhead electric travelling crane was installed above them. Notice the workshop area with machine tools still being installed. The wooden fence in the centre marks the prepared hole for the wheel drop – later used for the 'Atlas' wheel lathe. The hole in the floor just beyond the bay roads forms the foundation for a wheel lathe intended for axle journal turning of steam locomotives wheels – in the event this lathe was never installed.

The workshop area with the LMS-designed 1,600hp diesel 10001, clearly posed along with an EE Type 1 (later Class 20) and the diesel multiple units seen in the other views. Just to the left of the driver standing in front of 10001 is the hydraulic press for pushing out motion bushes for remetalling – it was never used for such work, until it was taken to the South shed when North shed closed. The large radial arm drill to the left also later 'migrated South'.

installed at Crewe North in late 1959 with fuel storage capacity of 60,000 gallons. Up till then all diesel servicing had been catered for at the South shed, using the equipment originally installed pre-war for the diesel shunters. Of course there were not many diesels about prior to the arrival of the EE and BR Type 4s – just the two LMS prototypes 10000-1, and the ex-Southern trio, 10201-3.

Originally main line diesels were maintained on a 'miles run' basis, with the exception of a 'Daily exam' as it was known, to check oil levels and the like. Later, hours run by the diesel engine were substituted as a more accurate measure, but the number of hours run were always calculated from the diagrams the locomotives worked rather than being accurately monitored. The 'A' exam was then undertaken at a 24-32 hour periodicity, with more detailed examinations at 125-150 hours, 500-600 hours (this one replaced the former 20,000-24,000 mile exam) and over the years these periodicities were gradually extended and designated A-B-C and so on up to E. The 125-150, for example, became the B exam.

I was transferred to Crewe Diesel from Crewe North and started there on Monday 31 August 1964. This was after a two-week holiday, one week of which was spent with a fellow apprentice in the Isle of Man. In those days two weeks holiday was all one got! I had finished at Crewe North on Friday 10 August, and the last locomotive I worked on was 44678, a Class 5 4-6-0 mixed traffic locomotive undergoing a No.6 mileage examination. During that last week I also worked on, from Monday to Thursday: Britannia Pacific 70042 'X' examination and repairs, Stanier Pacific 46248 brake block change, 45595 (a 5XP as we called them, though they were actually officially Class 6 by this time) 'X' examination and repairs, 46251 'X' examination and repairs (another Class 8) and 70019 'X' and 7-9 week examinations and repairs (another Britannia). The first locomotive I worked on at the Diesel Depot was EE Type 4 D211, undergoing a 125-150 hours examination, and the Fitter I worked with for that first week was Frank Dawson (always known, and for reasons nobody, including Frank ever seemed to know, as 'Nunk'). The Foreman on duty was the redoubtable Fred Bayman, who I was destined to cross swords with on numerous occasions henceforth; indeed when I 'came out of my time', I was allocated to Fred's shift, but that is another story!

At this time, as I mentioned above, the Diesel Depot only undertook the larger examinations, 125-150 hours and upwards along with the heavier repairs to the locomotives, servicing being undertaken at the North and South sheds. Apart from the Crewe South diesel shunters, the EE Type 4s made up almost the entire workload, although Crewe North had a small allocation of 'Baby Sulzers' as we called them, the Derby-built Type 2s, later Class 24 and 25. It should be mentioned however, that all the 105 EE Type 4 locomotives allocated to the Western Lines of the LMR, came to Crewe for their 500-600 hour and larger examinations, the 'home' depots at Longsight, Camden, Edge Hill and Carlisle Upperby only undertaking the smaller examinations themselves. The shed was under the control of a Shed Master, at the time one Peter Rowledge, the well-known railway author and although Crewe-trained had been on the Western Region in the Cardiff District, whence he came to Crewe in May 1963. Although appointed in March he had to attend a number of courses. Peter had an assistant, Doug Fisher, who arrived from Carlisle in the spring of the following year.

Three Foremen covered the three shifts and there was a day shift Electrical Foreman (officially known as the District Electrical Foreman); this was Tom Cordin, from Glasgow. One of the three Foremen, Jean Stubbs – part-French hence his name – soon left for better things at Buxton, taking charge of the new diesel multiple unit depot there, with the result that Fred Bayman and colleague Bill Lewis covered the job on a 12-hour rotating basis. Bill incidentally, had been the first salaried grade supervisor at the depot, when his job was a day turn only, with the other shifts covered by Leading Fitters, of which Fred Bayman was one. As no servicing was undertaken at that time the whole place closed up at Saturday lunchtime – yes we worked Saturday mornings in those days – and although latterly there was often a Sunday day shift on overtime, it only really opened again for a 7.30 am start on Monday morning, with three shift cover from then until Saturday lunchtime. Most of the staff worked on the three-shift basis in the sequence days, nights and then afternoons, but there was a small regular day shift and the apprentices worked on the day shift only.

When it first opened and before any main line locomotives were around, the initial workload consisted of the diesel shunting locomotives from Crewe South, which soon moved in for their maintenance to take early advantage of the better conditions and facilities. Fitters Harry Brownridge and Fred Bayman came with them, and as we saw earlier Fred later became one of the Foreman. However, before that happened Charlie Oxley had arrived from Gorton (where he had been Mechanical Foreman) as the first Shed Master and soon Fred and Jean became Leading Fitters, with Bill Lewis from Chester as the first salaried supervisor. Later still, as we saw above, these three became the Foremen covering the three shifts. Roy Fearon, hitherto on the work-study side and originally from Edge Hill, eventually replaced Jean. Charlie Oxley went on to Immingham as Depot Manager and was followed as Shed Master by Bill Gilpin. Bill moved on to Leicester shortly after, when Peter Rowledge arrived. After periods on the Eastern and Southern Regions, Charlie was later to emigrate to New Zealand, and retired as Acting Chief Mechanical Engineer of the New Zealand Government Railway.

As the number of EE Type 4 locomotives increased, and hence the depot workload, more and more Fitters and support staff were transferred from the North and South sheds. The skilled men were given the choice on how they should be selected for transfer to diesel work and as the railway then, and to some extent now, operated very much on a seniority basis, in normal circumstances the older men would have transferred first. However, after a vote it was decided that whilst they would be given the opportunity by seniority, individuals could elect to remain on steam, and the younger men given the opportunity to move. In most cases this is what happened. In the main the older men elected to remain on steam, and for a goodly number this saw them through to retirement. However, a significant number still had a number of years service left when steam finally finished at Crewe in November 1967 and had then to be trained on the new traction. This was a difficult period, but in the traditional Crewe way of doing things, it was accomplished by both management and men exceptionally well, with mutual respect all round. Of course some of the older blokes training on diesels when in their sixties, had had a good number of us younger ones as their apprentices in earlier days! The other aspect that had to be addressed on the introduction of the diesels was the need for electricians, and this was solved by employing men already apprentice trained and introducing them to railway work. In the main these people came from the local electricity supply and support industry.

By my time there had been a number of small improvements and other changes to the depot. A set of four Matterson locomotive body-lifting jacks had been installed at the north end of No.5 road, for example, and the pit sides had been strengthened to accommodate them. By these means a locomotive body could be removed from its bogies to allow traction motor and wheel set renewal. Up till then, locos had either to be sent into Crewe Works for such attention, or the Crewe North 50 ton breakdown crane had to be summoned. The southern end of all the roads, including the bays at that end, had been equipped with lubricating oil dispensers and a room at the northern end of the building, on the east side, had been fitted out with equipment to clean and coat with new oil the air intake filters from the engine rooms.

Of the steam arrangements, like the Blacksmith and Coppersmith shops, white metal hearth and the rest, these were hardly used, as were the bulk of the machine tools – only the grinder, small drill and occasionally the smaller of the two centre lathes saw any use. However, the Atlas under floor wheel lathe worked almost continually, not only with the fleet of diesel locomotives but all sorts of others, including the AC electric locomotives, coaches and vans, DMUs, and on at least one occasion to my knowledge, a steam locomotive tender!

One job that remained awkward to undertake in the new Depot was the replacement of the pony truck springs on the Type 4s. This meant removal of

English Electric 2,700hp experimental gas turbine-mechanical locomotive GT3 outside No.7 road at the south end of the depot. This locomotive used modified BR Standard Class 5 frames, both engine and tender. It entered service in January 1961, initially between Crewe and Carlisle, being maintained by English Electric staff at Crewe – later in the year it migrated for further trials on the former Great Central section. This view would have been taken in the early months of 1961; it was in this area that a fuelling installation was later built to supplement the one on No.1 road. The GT3 tender carried not only the fuel, but also a Clayton steam generator for train heating purposes. (Jim Hardy)

Top left. Inside the shed on 1 June 1969, with Derby-Sulzer Type 2 (later Class 24) 5076 on the wheel lathe, with another of the class to the left. The rest are EE D400 class locomotives (later Class 50). All fifty of these were originally delivered new to Crewe for use on the Anglo-Scottish trains and in replacing the Brush-Sulzer Type 4s (later Class 47s) on these jobs, in their turn allowed further cascades, resulting in the final elimination of steam traction in this country. View looks towards the southern end of the shed.

Middle left. For the Investiture of Charles, as Prince of Wales at Caernarfon Castle on I July 1969, several special trains ran to take the Prince, other members of the Royal family, members of the armed forces and guests to the ceremony. Most but not all of these started their journeys from Euston; one for example, as was to be expected, came from Cardiff. At Crewe we seemed to take weeks getting the locomotives ready, including these two. EE Type 4 diesels D233 EMPRESS OF ENGLAND and D216 CAMPANIA, were the usual 'Royal' engines on the Midland Region at the time and were allocated to Crewe, and they were used to work the train with the Queen, Prince Charles and other 'senior' members of the Royal family from Euston to Caernarfon on the night of 30 June 1969. Here they are outside the north end of the shed at 05.30 on the morning of 30 June, prior to working light to Willesden ready to work the Royal Train that same night.

Bottom left. Fine body of men posed in front of the Royal locomotives on the morning of 30 June; the night shift about to go home. Left to right: Allan Baker Fitter, Dick Roberts Fitter, Barry Harding Fitter, George Browness Fitter, Dave Morgan Fitter, Tony Hope Fitter, George Barber Fitter, 'Dan' Archer, Fitter's Mate, Charlie Skelling Fitter's Mate, Fred Roberts Fitter, Ted Owen Fitter's Mate, Ossie Jones Fitter, Les Surridge Fitter, Bob Dutton Fitter's Mate, Alec Watt Electrician and, on the steps of the locomotive, Roy – I cannot recall his surname, an Electrician. Despite the line being electrified between Crewe and London, diesels were always used on the Royal Train at this time as the Royal Train coaches were steam heated, and none of the electric locomotives were equipped to provide steam heat. The use of two locomotives was necessary not to provide cover for breakdowns as is often thought, but because of the steam heating boiler water tank capacity, so that stops would not have to be made en-route to take on water, instead the crews would change over the operating boiler from one locomotive to the other as the water ran out. The cable sticking up on the nose end door (beyond Barry Harding's right ear) is a part of the temporary telephone connection used to provide communication between the two locomotives and the train. Prior to the advent of mobile phones and other more sophisticated communication systems, this was standard practice for Royal trains. The equipment was kept in a large box with the coaches, and despatched to whatever depot was preparing the locomotives.

the pony truck wheels themselves and as the 2½ ton cranes were of insufficient capacity to lift the end of a complete bogie (after the body had been lifted clear by means of the Matterson jacks) the work was undertaken at the North shed on the wheel drop. The springs were of the conventional laminated leaf type and by these means it was possible to drop the pony wheels out of the way and gain access to the springs. This was a pretty lousy job and a frequent one, and we would be sent with the errant locomotive to the North shed to do it. The spring top plate was later re-designed with wrap-round rolled eyes to take the spring bolts, replaced by ones having eyes forged with the plate itself. This almost completely eliminated failure of these components, much to everyone's relief!

We had a whole plethora of diesel shunting locomotives to maintain, including of course the 350-400HP 0-6-0s (later the ubiquitous Class 08-9) which we then referred to as 'Twin Motors', as they had two traction motors, one each on the leading and trailing axles. The earlier ex-LMS jackshaft drive design had only a single motor, mounted in the locomotive body and driving the six-coupled wheels by jackshaft. Hence the term 'Twin Motor' for the subsequent design. These two classes by and large caused us few problems, but as for the rest! There were, I recall, three of the North British (NBL) 0-4-0s with a MAN engine and hydraulic transmission (D2909-2911), a solitary Hudswell Clarke 0-6-0 with Gardner engine and five-speed 'Wilson' epicyclic gearbox (D2519, soon joined by sister D2518) and several of the Drewry locomotives. These had been built by either Vulcan Foundry or Robert Stephenson & Hawthorns, in both cases under licence from Drewry with the same power train configuration as the Hudswell Clarke. Later we also got a few of the BR Swindon-built variants of the Drewry design.

Putting aside the fact that the Gardner engine types were frequently overloaded and not as well driven as they deserved to be, they caused us little trouble in so far as their design and manufacture was concerned, but the NBL locomotives were a real pain. The MAN six cylinder 330hp turbo-charged engine and Voith gearbox had been built under licence by North British but without, it appeared, the accuracy and tender loving care bestowed by the licence holders, with the result that they were in almost constant trouble. In fairness it has to be said that they were far too powerful for the amount of tractive effort (at 25% adhesion no less than 20,160lb!) the rather large wheels were able to put down, with the not surprising result of overheated transmissions and the like. Most of the shunter maintenance was undertaken at weekends, hence one of the reasons for the Sunday day shift but it was quite usual to find a number of them 'left over', to confront us on Monday mornings and it would be mid-week before we saw the back of them all! This would of course, often result in some of the jobs they worked having to be covered by steam engines and the Control Office would be constantly on the phone chasing our projected release times. Many of these shunting diagrams were single manned and the drivers were men on light duties for medical reasons. The result of non-availability was that these jobs would have to be covered by 'sets' of spare men, or men from other links with all the rostering disruption this caused – happy days indeed!

One of the interesting distractions were what were termed 'call outs', where we would be sent to attend to the malfunctioning of some locomotive or other, and shunting locomotives were often involved. Now these were spread all over Crewe, and as we usually walked it could take a long time! For example a locomotive employed at the southern end of Basford Hall marshalling yards meant a three-mile walk there and back. We were also regularly called to attend main line locomotives in the station area along with DMUs both there and at the carriage shed, where one of our Fitter's Mates used to go over and fuel and water those sets diagrammed for such attention. Later, when diesel shunters took over the shunting jobs in Crewe Works, we used to get called out for them too, and in this case we generally got the van to fetch and carry us, but it was not unknown to catch the bus, getting some petty cash from the clerks first!

Many of the shunting jobs, as I said earlier, were covered by elderly drivers eking out their last years on light duties, and there were some cantankerous fellows among them! If they were used to a 'Twin Motor' and got a Drewry, or even worse one of the NBLs, they would find all sorts of things wrong with a view to getting it changed for something else. I have known weeks when we would be called out to the same locomotive and driver almost every day, and for a variety of niggling little 'nothings'! But it was good for the pocket, because we got a call out allowance on every occasion. Occasionally we would be called further afield to locomotives in trouble on the main line, when the van would always be used, and to the two Drewry locomotives that worked at Stafford (these were later replaced by 'Twin Motors'). This latter would be a whole day job, accompanied by a 'liquid lunch' in some local hostelry!

The EE Type 4s were good to work on, with plenty of room around all the major components and in all fairness they gave us little trouble. Among the bigger jobs we undertook and which occurred occasionally were traction motor and wheel set renewal, and leaking cylinder liner joints, which allowed engine coolant to leak into the lubricating oil sump – not a good idea! This latter job would require removal of the cylinder head, piston and liner, as well as renewal of the filters and washing out the residual water from the engine sump.

On the more extensive 3000-3600 hour exams the turbo chargers were renewed with a serviced set and the fuel injectors were changed. The earlier locomotives had a different arrangement of injector fuel and spill pipes, with the result that they were frequently in trouble with fuel oil dilution of the lubricating oil. Later engines had what were called anti-dilution trays, which were designed to ensure that if there were leaks the leaking fuel did not get to the sump – they were moderately successful and I think the earlier engines were later modified to this arrangement. Another rather big job was the renewal of the cam shaft drive chain and getting it wrong could have serious consequences. The twin camshafts were driven by a three-link side-by-side roller chain and until a 'fret-free' one was developed these chains, due to stretch, had to be renewed at the 3000-3600 hour exam. It was a tricky job with the engine in situ, and very easy to get one or other cylinder bank timing wrong, with the result that the chain would have to come off again! The fret-free chain had a different design of rollers to prevent such a high wear rate and came about after a chain broke on D308 when it was working a Royal Train with the Queen herself on board – this was in August 1963 at Law Junction and the train was en-route to Aberdeen.

All the locomotives of course, had steam heating boilers of one sort or another, in the case of the Type 4s, either a Stone OK4625 or a Clayton RO2500; both were of the water tube 'flash' type. In actual fact they were steam generators rather than boilers as such. Now these items of equipment were without doubt the Achilles heel of diesel traction in its early days on passenger working, and whilst in general terms they would work away merrily statically, when rattled around at speeds up to 90 mph on a locomotive this was far from the case! Routine maintenance, especially on the Stone units, was quite straightforward, but fault finding on either unit was fraught with difficulty, particularly the Clayton as this was far more complicated electrically! Built under licence by EE at the Vulcan Foundry, if the combustion was not set and maintained to perfection, the coil unit would get successively blocked with soot with disastrous consequences – on this boiler the firing head was at the bottom of the coil unit, whilst on the Stone it was at the top. It has to be said that the boilers were neglected by the crews; steam

Top left. With the introduction of the summer timetable on 5 April 1970, the Anglo-Scottish trains were considerably speeded up, both south and north of Crewe. To effect the accelerations north, it was decided to use the EE 2,700hp D400s in multiple, two to each of six trains each way, five to and from London and one to and from Birmingham. This picture taken on the first day shows D437 leading and D447 behind, about to leave the shed to work the inaugural down accelerated 'Royal Scot' north of Crewe, which had left Euston at 10.00am that morning. The characters left to right are Fitters Tony Hope, David Owen and Barry Harding. View looks south from the north end of the shed.

Middle left. Taken on the same occasion as the previous view and showing in front of the locomotive and from left to right: Fitters Barry Harding, David Owen, Fred Roberts and yours truly.

Bottom left. The experimental 4,000hp diesel electric KESTREL, built by Brush as a speculative venture, never caught on with BR and eventually Hawker Siddeley, the owners of Brush, sold it to the Russian Railways. Crewe Works prepared it for shipment from Cardiff Docks and because the bogies had been converted to the Russian gauge of 5 feet, it was necessary to borrow a pair of Class 47 bogies to move it by rail to the docks. Its own bogies by the way, were loaded on the flat wagons for the journey and it was reunited with them before loading on to the ship. The locomotive is at Crewe Diesel Depot waiting movement to Cardiff on 4 June 1971. Left to right are: Fitters Les Surridge, David Owen and Dave Morgan, followed by a Fitter's Mate whose name escapes me, Shop Office man Harry Steele, and Foremen Ken Parker and Fred Bayman.

locomotive Fireman in particular became very lazy once they got on the diesels, and it was obvious that in many cases they were not undertaking the soot blowing and proper shut down procedures that they were instructed to, and this in itself caused many of the problems.

From late 1964 the first Brush-Sulzer Type 4s (later Class 47) were allocated to Crewe North and I noted that the first one I actually worked on was D1632, undergoing a 125-150 hour exam on 2 February 1965, followed by D1634 for a similar exam on 18 February. Meantime the staple diet of EE Type 4s continued and I did not work on another 'Brush' as we called them then, until 20 April – this was D1631, also a 125-150 hour exam. However, by the middle of the year they were becoming much more prevalent, as more and more of the class were allocated to Crewe and as bigger and bigger inroads were made into the steam allocation. A sizeable fleet of the Derby-designed Sulzer Type 2s (later

Class 24 and 25) were drafted in too.

In early 1965 a decision was taken to close Crewe North shed, transferring the remaining steam complement to Crewe South. Diesel servicing and smaller examinations would be done at the Diesel Depot. Prior to this taking place some quite major alterations were undertaken. First of all the fuel storage tank capacity at the Diesel Depot had to be increased and two of the tanks were transferred from the North shed. Alterations were made inside the Depot, including a partial screen between Nos.1 and 2 roads in an attempt to reduce the amount of exhaust fumes that would penetrate the main part of the shed, as No.1 road was to be used for the servicing 'A' exams and light repairs. In effect, it would become a 'running' road. Extra fume extraction equipment was installed over this road too.

By way of improving facilities for steam at the South shed, which had always relied on its North shed 'big brother' to help it out with wheel drop work, bigger mileage examinations and so on, the larger and almost unused machine tools from the Diesel Shed were transferred there. All these machines were of course in much better condition than those at the North shed, indeed they had hardly been used; clearly it was better to use them rather than transfer the aged equipment from the North shed. In April 1965 Peter Rowledge moved on to the Stoke Divisional Office, with Doug Fisher taking over his position. Bob Capewell replaced Doug, Bob coming from Barrow where he had been Shed Master, although he was Crewe trained and was in effect, 'returning home'.

Although the South shed had a wheel drop, as it was operated by a steam donkey engine it had largely fallen out of use in favour of the newer one at the North shed where the operating hydraulic machinery was driven by electric motor. This was despite the fact that even the North shed machinery dated back to pre-grouping LNWR days; it still had an LNWR cast iron plant number plate on it! As an interesting aside, until improved lifting facilities were available at the Diesel Depot, which as we shall see were soon in coming, any pony truck spring changes after the North shed drop table was taken out of use had to be done at the South shed. This demanded some lengthy preparation as first of all we had to get up steam on the vertical boiler, which had been repaired and re-commissioned, and all this provided great entertainment for us apprentices! Later on it was kept in steam most of the time as I recall, and served as a warm place in the winter where we used to congregate – there was no shed heating otherwise!

Other improvements at the Diesel Depot included making use of the area previously occupied by the machine tools and Nos.7 and 8 bay roads at the south end were extended over this area, without pits. Indeed, No.6 pit was filled in and these alterations not only gave accommodation for two more locomotives, but also provided a concreted area in which it was intended a 6 ton road crane could operate. A crane of this capacity would be capable of lifting one end of a bogie to enable us to change those dreaded pony springs, as well as lifting out train heating boilers and other large items beyond the capacity of the overhead cranes. In the event this was not all that successful as manoeuvring the crane in the confined area proved troublesome. Most lifting was therefore undertaken outside the shed, usually on the concrete apron at the north end which was later extended to better facilitate this type of work. Prior to this we had used the breakdown crane, then kept at the North shed, for the occasional lifting job, including train-heating boilers. But it was a lengthy operation by these means.

Along with these changes No.5 road at the south end was strengthened and second set of Matterson jacks introduced, so that henceforth two locomotives could be lifted simultaneously. All this of course made the place much, much busier, and staffing levels were increased along with more messing and office facilities. As locomotives were still to be stabled at what was left of the North shed yard, because there was insufficient space to stable many locomotives at the Diesel Depot, a second connection was made to the main lines, in this case to the up Chester Independent line west of the depot, connected to the depot run-round road. There was an associated crossover to the down Chester Independent, to enable traffic to proceed northwards. Controlled by Salop Goods Junction signal box, by this route locomotives were ferried, usually in twos and threes, to what became the North Holding Sidings, established partly on the site of the North shed. This had actually closed on and from 24 May 1965, and the new arrangements came into use the following day, a Sunday. It should be mentioned here that, prior to movement of the diesel servicing from the North shed, the work was undertaken by staff from the Diesel Depot, on a rota basis, three-week stints at a time covering one week on each of the three shifts. Two Fitters and two Fitter's Mates were employed at any one time, under the control of the North shed Leading Fitter; one Mate would be employed on fuelling duties and the other assisting the Fitters.

As mentioned earlier with the increased workloads came increases in staffing levels. More and more men transferred from steam and others were recruited externally – often men previously railway trained in the Works, so that training requirements and problems of 'culture clash' were reduced. Some however, came from Rolls Royce, the other sizeable engineering employer in Crewe and of course the differences from building Rolls Royce cars to maintaining railway locomotives were quite significant!

There were also increases in supervision, as it was soon realised that management of the day to day locomotive servicing requirements, including 'A' exams and minor repairs, was too much to be managed by one Foreman on shifts. Three additional positions were created to cover this workload with a separate group of staff undertaking the work, albeit on a rotating basis with the remainder. This work continued to be described after the fashion of steam days, the 'Y' scheme as opposed to 'X' scheme. The men on this work were therefore, henceforth known as 'The Y Men', and the type of work as 'Wise'. Old traditions died hard at Crewe! The initial appointments to these positions were Ken Parker, previously a member of the work study team, and originally from Edge Hill, together with Cliff Walker and on a temporary basis John Plevin, both Crewe men. Later Stan Kimberlin took over from John. Stan had been the Mechanical Foreman at Crewe South, John moving on to become one of the Ultrasonic Axle Testing Inspectors. These were new positions for the axle testing introduced nation-wide about this time, and Barry Harding joined him, another Crewe trained man.

As well as this and to help with the intricacies and foibles of diesel traction, salaried grade Technical Inspectors were appointed to cover the shifts, and the job of ultrasonically testing axles (mentioned above) was also covered by men in salaried positions. One of the first Inspector appointments was Brian Heath, who came from the Electric Traction Depot; others were Harry Bradley and Gordon Moore.

Some time later, in 1969, a 'load bank' was installed at the south end of the depot with a dedicated spur off No.1 road being laid to serve it. The equipment enabled locomotive diesel engines, generators and load control systems to be tested statically, by disconnecting the traction motors and connecting the generator to a resistance bank. Further Inspectors were appointed to cover locomotives either undergoing load test due to faults, or running in after engine component changes – pistons, cylinder liners and the like. Extra accommodation had to be provided for these people, and the office arrangements at the north end of the depot were extended and re-arranged to suit. There were also further enlargements to the staff messing and locker facilities at the opposite, south end of the depot, along with car parking. In many cases locomotives employed on freight duties continued to stable on the South shed between jobs and fuelling facilities were retained for these as well as the shunters. Crewe South closed to steam on Saturday 5 November 1967 but again, like the North shed, the site was retained for stabling purposes. However, this mismatch of servicing facilities and detached stabling points was most unsatisfactory, and plans were developed for a major remodelling. The scheme consisted of converting the Old Yard, to the immediate east of the Diesel Depot and used for all types of traffic using non-passenger carrying coaching stock, parcel traffic and the like, into a purpose-built locomotive fuelling, servicing and stabling yard. There was ample capacity for all the anticipated locomotive servicing and stabling requirements. The South shed site was to be cleared and remodelled with ten new sidings so as to allow traffic hitherto handled at the Old Yard to be dealt with there. Lastly, the site of the North shed was to be completely vacated.

These new arrangements came into use, without a hitch, at 06.00 on Monday 3 August 1970. From this date all locomotives came onto the Diesel Depot by a connection from the down Salop line at the south end of the depot. According on what attention they needed they were directed to either the Diesel Depot itself or the Holding Sidings. Later, in December 1970, a locomotive washing plant was brought into use in the new sidings. One road was reserved for the breakdown train and as it was still steam powered its special needs had to be provided for; hitherto, it had remained at the South shed where it had migrated when the North shed closed. Incidentally, Ralph Blunt who had been Shed Master at Crewe South and temporarily at Crewe North in its latter days, moved to the Diesel Depot on closure taking over the position held by Bill Lewis, who had unfortunately died in harness in the early summer of 1966. Ralph was Doncaster trained, and went on to become Train Crewe Manager at Chester, where Bob Capewell later joined him as Depot Engineer.

By this time the fleets of locomotives maintained at the Diesel Depot had been augmented by the English Electric 'Type 4½', the 2,700HP (later Class 50s) D400s, the entire fifty being allocated to Crewe for the Anglo Scottish trains, as a last attempt to improve this service prior to electrification. They got the unofficial appellation '4½' because their horsepower fell roughly halfway between the Type 4 EE 2,000HP locos and the 3,300HP Type 5 Deltics. My notes tell me that the first of the class, D400, had its first 175-200 hour examination on 4 October 1967, with D401 following on 8 December. From the summer timetable of 1970, introduced on 4 May, these locomotives worked the Anglo-Scottish services in multiple in an attempt to improve the timings. As I recall there were six such workings each way each day, five to and from London and one to and from Birmingham, with the D400s coming on and off the trains at Crewe. This arrangement continued even after the decision had been taken to electrify to Glasgow, as it allowed reasonable timings to be maintained during the disruption caused by the engineering works. It also of course, helped in case of one or other of the locomotives being in trouble, especially on the long single-track sections in use whilst electrification was underway.

During this period I spent a lot of time as an Acting Foreman at the Diesel Depot and I greatly enjoyed this part of my career and the experience gained. I used to particularly like the night shift in the summer, when it would get light around 3.30am, and working in close liaison with the Running Foreman to ensure he had enough 'power' to meet his commitments. Of course there were rough times with the smooth, and I recall spending the best part of one Boxing Day at Stafford trying to get the locomotives (stabled there over the holiday period) up and running again after a Christmas shut down, when it snowed to boot! We seemed to have colder winters in those days and I recall often having to clear fuel lines, both on the locomotives and the fixed installations, the diesel fuel having frozen.

I do not intend taking the story of Crewe Diesel Depot much further, as my involvement lessened when I moved to the Divisional Office at Stoke to take up an appointment as a Divisional Rolling Stock Inspector in July 1971. Whilst I still maintained a connection with the Depot during my period at Stoke, it was much less, and in September 1974 I moved south to London as Traction Maintenance Engineer at Finsbury Park Depot on the Eastern Region. The Depot at Crewe of course, went on to even greater things, and has survived until recently as a part of the EWS locomotive maintenance operations. Unfortunately, the loss of the Post Office traffic has resulted in a rationalisation of the EWS locomotive needs, with the result that the depot closed on and from 1 January 2004. There were some great blokes there, first class craftsman and real 'mates', and I will always have a great affection for Crewe Diesel Depot.

The south end of the Diesel Depot, looking north with the three bays and the run-round road to the left, 1 June 1985. Notice the three hip roofed sections, two three road ones flanking a central two road section. There are a large number of Sulzer engined Type 2s; they were a feature of the allocation for much of the 1970-80 period. From left to right the locomotives are 25202, 25298, 25297, 47234, 25229 and 25213. (GW Morrison)

Top right. Class 47 47355 lifted from its bogies by four Matterson jacks so that the bogies can receive attention, on No.5 road (south) on 27 February 1988. Alongside on No.6 road are Class 47s 47433 and 47436. This was the second of the jacking installations; the earlier one was at the opposite, north end of this road. The heavy rope in the skip to the right was for a series of capstans used to pull locomotives over the below ground level 'Atlas' wheel lathe. The old style rope and capstan arrangement meant that another locomotive would not be required every time the job moved on to the next wheelset. Shortly after this photograph was taken the wheel lathe here, by this time quite old, was removed and a new one installed at the nearby Electric Traction Depot. (GW Morrison)

Right. Class 37 37250 on 27 February 1988 at what had been the Down, or Old Yard, converted for locomotive servicing and stabling back in August 1970. The view is looking southwards with the locomotive leaving the washing plant; one of the fuel storage tanks is on the left. (GW Morrison)

The Diesel Depot looking due south, from the top of Rail House on the Nantwich Road, 27 February 1988. On the extreme left are the workshops of the Midland Roll Makers, the former North Staffordshire Railway line curving away past them to Stoke-on-Trent. Next to the right is the Carriage Shed, beyond the footbridge. In the foreground are the Independent lines and Salop Goods Junction signal box – note, to the left of these lines, the formation of the steeply inclined former Diesel Depot exit road. The main line south is to the upper right, and below it the South Yard, formerly site of the South shed, by this time used for non-passenger carrying coaching stock. This facility replaced the former Down Yard when it was handed over for conversion into locomotive servicing and stabling requirements. (Gavin Morrison)

Left. Crewe North Junction looking north with the extreme north end of No.4 Platform to the right and Crewe North 'Middle' shed to the left. This is the 1940 re-signalling scheme but no work on the actual signals appears to have started, although the new North Junction box can be seen in front of the old cabin. The apparatus above the signal, which is the No.1 Through Line starter, is an early form of route indicator. Notice the wagons of locomotive coal alongside the shed.

Below. A similar view but a little to the left and illustrating how one new colour light signal with route indicator could replace no less then four semaphore signals, the new gantry being erected in front of the old one. The route indicator has not yet been installed but can be seen on the gantry ready for installation. The footbridge across the north end of the platforms was for staff use and also gave access to the North shed. The large building on the extreme left at the end of the 'Middle' shed is the stores, seen earlier. Notice the Webb 2-4-2T and ex-LNWR brake van; this would be the 'Rag Mail' engine and brake – see Chapter One. The small hut to the right is for a fog hand signalman.

Chapter Three

Points and Signals

It could well surprise readers that one of the most extensive and indeed ambitious re-signalling schemes introduced by the LMS, in its entire existence no less, took place during the early years of the Second World War, in 1940 in fact, and where else but Crewe? Why was this so, and how did the Company manage it? The reasons are two-fold. First, in view of the extent of the scheme, plans had in fact been put in hand well before hostilities commenced; design work had been started and much of the new equipment ordered. Secondly, as the old equipment was becoming life-expired it was increasing difficult for Crewe to be able to handle all the traffic asked of it. Not only were there regular breakdowns in the old equipment but even at its best it could not manage the increased movements consequent upon the war effort. The decision was consequently made to go ahead with the scheme despite the obvious disruption that would be caused whilst the changes were made. But once put in hand so to speak, schemes of this magnitude are difficult if not impossible to stop.

The equipment to be replaced dated from the period 1897-1907 and in its day was both innovative and unique. In 1897 the famous LNWR Locomotive Superintendent F.W. Webb (later Chief Mechanical Engineer) along with the Company's Signal Superintendent A.M. Thompson designed, developed and eventually patented (May 1897) a system of signalling henceforth to be known as the 'Crewe System'. It was power operated, making the LNWR a pioneer in this form of signalling and thus the initial installation at Crewe was not only the first power operated system in this country, but it would appear the first electrically operated one in the world.

Other power operated systems, notably in the USA, used either compressed air or hydraulic power as operating medium and the North American Westinghouse Company and its offshoot British Westinghouse were, of course, instrumental in developments using compressed air. It is said (however true this might be I cannot say) that Webb was totally against the use of compressed air on the Westinghouse system as he was still 'smarting' over his defeat by that company in the famous brake trials of 1875. In that year, it will be recalled, his favoured Clark-Webb chain brake was stoutly defeated by the Westinghouse air brake! Be that as it may, we have ample evidence of Webb's willingness to experiment and of course, as the LNWR generated its own electricity at Crewe, power supplies were readily available for such a system. Hydraulic power, by the way, wherein water was the medium, was discounted in the light of potential frost damage in winter – this was despite its wide application by the LNWR elsewhere at Crewe.

The 'Crewe System' was first put into use at Crewe Gresty Lane signal cabin (the LNWR always used the word cabin, as opposed to box which was in more common use by other railways) to control a series of new connecting spurs from the line to Shrewsbury and just to the west of Crewe South Junction. At this time the layout at Crewe was undergoing great changes to enable it to handle the ever increasing traffic. Principal among these was a complex of avoiding lines so that trains not requiring the station itself could bypass it completely. They became known as the Independent lines (mentioned several times already) and connected all three of the routes north, that is to Chester, Liverpool and the north, and Manchester, directly with the extended marshalling yards at Basford Hall south of the station. They also formed a through route, reconnecting with the main line south at Basford Hall Junction. The new spurs at Gresty Lane provided connections between the

Photograph taken from almost the identical spot as the previous one and after completion of the re-signalling. Notice the old signal cabin has been demolished along with the fog signalman's hut. The large building to the right distance is the Oil & Grease Recovery Works, where the oil and grease recovered in the workshops was recycled.

View inside the old North Junction cabin showing the Webb-Thompson frames with one set of miniature levers over the other. As well as the block instruments on the block shelf, there are a number of circular signal position indicators. On the extreme right of the block shelf is a circular route indicator and a bell to indicate to 'A' cabin a movement to the Horse Landing.

Shrewsbury line and the Independent lines, which passed in a deep cutting west of the station.

The installation at Gresty Lane (later Gresty Lane No.1) consisted of a revolutionary miniature 57 lever arrangement with the levers in twin rows, one above the other. There were two 'sets', each with 19 levers, 10 in the

Looking south from the Manchester line with a new colour light signal installation already in position and the old semaphore gantry behind – one colour light and route indicator replacing nine semaphores. Notice that the old gantry also carries the down advanced starter along with the distant for Sydney Bridge Junction, the next box to the north-east. Again, its colour light replacement is in position (on the right) although control of Sydney Bridge Junction passed to the North Junction box on completion of the works. Old and new signal boxes can be seen, and, to the extreme right, the top of the tunnel carrying the Independent lines. The 'Middle' shed is in the distance, Up Hill Sidings to left and, to extreme right, part of the Oil & Grease Works.

From the same position as the previous shot, on completion of the works. Note how much clearer the view was for enginemen. The signal is showing a clear aspect with the route set for Platform 6.

top row and nine in the bottom. The space required per lever was much less than a conventional lever frame, so the size of the cabin was less than half of what would otherwise be the case. There were of course, no wires or rods protruding from the cabin but a conventional tappet type of mechanical interlocking was used with the electrical switches controlling the signal and point motors located below the locking mechanism. It is believed that this was the first use of the tappet principle of mechanical interlocking on the LNWR, the Webb Patent 'Tumbler' type predominating elsewhere on the system together with other earlier types.

The point controlling levers embodied what was called a 'check lock' position which ensured that the points had fully responded and been detected, before the lever could be pulled fully home and any related interlocking released. At 110volts relatively high amperages were required to control the point motors (originally these were magnet operated units, later replaced by conventional rotary motors) and solenoid signal motors. All the signals, incidentally, were still of the semaphore type but with electric lamps rather than oil lamps, which could be switched on and off by the signalman to save electricity in daytime. Conventional paraffin signal lamps were of course alight all the time.

The whole was an extremely neat and compact arrangement, greatly relieving the load of the signalman. At the same time and perhaps, from the Company's point of view more importantly, it allowed much faster operation of the layout, at a reduced cost in maintenance – there were no wires and rods to frequently adjust for example. It was brought into use in January 1899.

As with most things LNWR the entire installation was made by the Company in its own workshops, in this case at Crewe Works, as was of course the existing Webb 'Tumbler' equipment. Success of the Gresty Lane installation led to further developments and in connection with the marshalling yard extensions and Independent lines a new cabin was erected at Salop Goods Junction. A 57-lever frame similar to

View looking south from the main line to the north with the Oil & Grease Works to the left and the Old Works Yard to the right – notice the locomotives stabled outside the old No.1 Erecting Shop which was by this date the 'home' of the Works Pilots. It is unusual, therefore, to see a 2-6-4T there. Observe no less than twenty-one semaphore arms, although six of the distants are 'fixed'. On the extreme right is a distant signal for trains in the down direction, in this case it is the distant for Crewe Coal Yard, the next box north. On the extreme right can just be seen a fog signalman's hut complete with brazier. The footbridge was to give access from the Main Works to the Oil & Grease Works.

Taken from almost the same position as the previous view and showing the twin colour lights and route indicators that have replaced the large array of semaphores. The right-hand signal is showing a double amber aspect with the route set to Platform 4. Note that the old gantry is still standing, albeit devoid of any signals. The twin semaphores to the left of the new gantry are the up home and distant for Salop Goods Junction on the down Liverpool Independent line, itself at a lower level and out of sight as it is about to go into a tunnel under the North Junction. Because of the distance these signals were from Salop Goods Junction box, which controlled them, these signals were motor operated.

the one at Gresty Lane, it was brought into use in March 1901. Others followed: Sorting Sidings South, 76 levers introduced in June 1901, Sorting Sidings Middle, 152 levers introduced in August 1901 and Sorting Sidings North, 95 levers introduced in October 1901.

In these cases and all future installations the voltage was increased to 200, with a consequent reduction in amperage as the high current used by the motors with 110 volts had caused some problems. As well as the layout improvements already mentioned, the station was increased in size by the addition of a new island to the west of the existing platforms. Designated Nos.1 and 2 platform faces, their installation involved a consequent renumbering of the other platforms. Along with the demolition of one of the North shed buildings this work necessitated completely new junction arrangements to the north and south of the station. The demolition of the first of the North shed buildings left the later oddly named 'Middle Shed' in 'the middle' of nothing – as described more fully in Chapter One.

Two new signal cabins, equipped on the new principles, were built for the station extensions, at the North and South Junctions. The North Junction cabin had 266 levers, again arranged in two tier sets of 19 levers each (i.e. 38 per set). Because of the 'Spider' bridge which connected the station with the Works, the frames were divided into two separate lots so as to allow the bridge deck to pass through the base of the cabin. This cabin came into use on 5th November 1906, replacing a mechanical cabin with 144 levers dating in turn from 1878. The new island platform came into use at the same time.

The South Junction cabin was opened in June 1907. It had 247 levers; once again, the frames were split in half, but in this case to give access to the windows for cleaning purposes rather than the bridge deck as at the North

With the re signalling works under way this view looks north-west along the Chester line, with the Old Works to the right and the North shed yard to the left. From right to left in the background can be seen the Old Works Stores, Signal Shop and, above it, the Old Works forge chimney and the tower of Christ Church. The large building to the extreme left is the Outstation Locomotive Stores, from where locomotive parts were despatched to sheds all over the system. These would be engines for which Crewe had repair responsibility; this would mean more or less all the locomotives at a solidly 'LNW' shed like Nuneaton, say, or Camden. For a shed like Polmadie it would be only the big passenger types – Pacifics and Royal Scots and not much else. There would be other sheds, in Scotland or on the Midland lines, or former L&Y sheds, which sent no engines to Crewe for repairs, or very few.

From almost the same spot as the previous view, after the re-signalling. Once again we see how much clearer the outlook is for engine crews. The 'Super D' 0-8-0 is hauling a string of engines off Works, destined for the South shed. All ex-works engines (the Crewe term was 'Fresh Off Works', abbreviated to FOW) went first of all to the South shed where they were lit up and moved to the North shed for running in if passenger or mixed traffic types. Otherwise they went straight to their home sheds.

Junction. This cabin replaced two earlier ones, one at the South Junction itself on the opposite up side of the main line and another, the South Station Signal Cabin, between what became 3 and 4 platforms.

As well as North Junction and South Junction, two smaller installations were necessary, one to control the crossovers between the new No.1 platform and the new down No.1 through line, together with access to the Horse Dock, and a second one between what became Nos.2 and 3 platforms. The former, 'A' cabin, had 26 levers and was situated to the west of platform 1 at the northern end of the station; it came into use in February 1907. The second, commissioned on the same date, was known as 'B' cabin, and had 26 levers. Interestingly these two cabins had flat roofs with twin single tier frames of 13 levers each, mounted side by side. Retained from the earlier arrangement was the Scissors Crossing Signal Cabin, an overhead affair straddling the gap between what became platforms 4 and 5 and just north of the over bridge carrying the Nantwich Road. The 'A' cabin of 1907, complete with its equipment, survives today as a part of the Crewe Heritage Centre.

Following the success of these arrangements at Crewe, further installations utilising the same principles were put into use, between Euston and Camden in 1905, and Manchester London Road in 1908-9, with a further one at Camden itself, in 1920. Euston station was not modernised however, and it was left to BR in the early 1950s to replace the mechanical equipment in use there.

As one of the busiest junctions in the country it will come as no surprise to find the equipment at Crewe well worn by the late 1930s, and for its replacement to be under consideration by the LMS. We are fortunate that despite the onset of the Second World War and before work actually started, the LMS arranged for a comprehensive photographic record of the old equipment, together with its replacements. Because of the great strategic importance of the installations where the Webb-Thompson equipment was in use, a

Looking along the Chester line but in the opposite direction from the two previous views, before the re-signalling was complete. Notice the new signal box just discernible next to the old one, and the entrance to the Works Yard to the left. Crewe North shed to right with the *Crewe Arms Hotel* looming in the centre.

Top left. **Almost the same vantage point but a little further south; the old signal cabin has been demolished, though as can be seen, its substantial base remained, and does so to this day. The new colour light signal shows a clear aspect and the route is set for Platform 3 – notice the signal box is camouflage painted. The *Crewe Arms Hotel* is again prominent, to the right of the box.**

Middle and bottom left. **Inside the new North Junction box, showing the electric miniature frames, all-electric diagram, conventional block instruments and route indicators, and the Regulator's desk. Note too, the illuminated indicator to show the signalmen what trains were in the platforms. This installation still exists, albeit not operational any more, as a part of the Crewe Heritage Centre.**

decision was taken early in the war years to remove it from two of the Crewe cabins, Salop Goods Junction and Sorting Siding South, to make spares available for the other installations. The equipment recovered from Crewe North and South Junctions later augmented this stockpile of spares. It should be remembered that it would have been virtually impossible to manufacture new equipment of this type, particularly at that dark period. Interestingly, the two cabins where the equipment was replaced had to be doubled in size to accommodate a standard LMS mechanical frame! These mechanical frames of course, were also built at Crewe.

It is perhaps worth mentioning in passing that the LNWR was the only one of the pre-grouping railway companies to manufacture its own signalling equipment in such a comprehensive manner and an extensive, specialised Signal Shop existed in the Old Works. This practice continued in LMS days and indeed into BR times, with Crewe Works finally ceasing to manufacture signalling equipment in the mid-1960s.

The new equipment at the two junctions came into use in the latter part of 1940, the North box being commissioned on 25 August. It consisted of a complete electrical installation with electrical interlocking and colour light signals controlled by Westinghouse miniature lever frames. Of the new signal boxes (the LMS favoured 'box' rather than 'cabin'!) the one at the North Junction was built in front of the old cabin; at the South Junction it was on the opposite, up side of the main line. Both were of reinforced concrete construction, of modern if austere appearance and with supposedly bombproof flat roofs. At the same time some alterations were made to 'A' cabin; colour light signals replaced the semaphores but the Webb-Thompson frame remained. Both 'B' and the Scissors Crossing cabins were abolished and their operations transferred to the new Junction boxes.

The other Crewe installations of the Webb-Thompson equipment, at Sorting Sidings Middle and North boxes, were left until eventually replaced as part of the 1961 modernisation of the Marshalling Yard. The North box gave way to an illuminated switch panel and the Middle box to a completely new box with similar equipment. In fact the operations of the Middle cabin were divided into two, new Middle Up and Middle Down signal boxes; as the names suggest, these were on opposite sides of the enlarged yard.

The station 'A' cabin and Gresty Lane No.1 survived with their Webb-Thompson equipment until the massive remodelling of Crewe undertaken between 2 June and 21 July 1985. This modernisation also replaced the North and South Junction boxes and their 1940 equipment, a new 'solid state' interlocking signalling centre being built on part of the site of the old North shed. However, both boxes still exist; North Junction, complete with all its equipment, has formed part of the Heritage Centre and the South Box, albeit devoid of its equipment, serves as an equipment store.

As we saw earlier, 'A' cabin was removed to a site within the Heritage Centre, and is now available for public inspection. Incidentally, the famous 'Spider bridge' had been dismantled prior to the 1940 rationalisation. The narrow gauge railway (18 inch) for internal Works traffic had run over this bridge to gain access to the station, in this case to take spare locomotive material to and from the station for onward transport to and from the outlying sheds – the railway had fallen out of use in 1932. After this the bridge was used by the replacement self-propelled rubber tyred Works internal transport, but it too, ceased to use the bridge in 1939. Thereafter, when necessary, the material was transported to and from the station in either standard gauge vehicles or road motors.

Before closing this Chapter it is perhaps worth mentioning that right until the end of the British Railways Board's existence under the terms of the Railway Act 1993, the Signal & Telecommunications Department maintained extensive workshops at Gresty Lane in Crewe, and not only was equipment repaired there, but a manufacturing facility existed too. Indeed, the signalling switch panels for the works in connection with the 1961 Marshalling Yard improvements were made there. This workshop now belongs to National Rail Suppliers Limited (NRS), a member of the Unipart Group of Companies and it continues to both maintain and manufacture signalling equipment, and not only for the national rail system in this country, but elsewhere in the world too.

Panorama during the re-signalling works, from the top of the new all-concrete North Junction box showing the north junction with the station beyond. The 3F shunting tank to left would be the Up Hill Siding engine, often referred to as the 'Bank Engine'; the *Crewe Arms Hotel* is to centre left and the North shed to extreme right. Just to the left of the North shed can be seen the Independent lines as they emerge from the tunnel under the North Junction and pass south in a deep cutting.

View north with No.2 Platform to the left; one of the 3F tank station pilots has a rake of coaches – to the right of these is the station 'B' cabin, which was later replaced as a part of the re signalling works. Note new signal gantry already in position and No.3 platform behind the screen to right.

The same vantage point on completion of the works, but with 'B' cabin still in place. The train is a Great Western one and would have arrived from Wellington by the GWR route from Nantwich via Market Drayton; the engine will be a Wellington-based 2-6-2T.

Further north along No.2 platform for a good view of the diminutive 'B' cabin. The substantial wall to the right separated this side of the station from the remainder; it was of course originally the outer wall of the station, before the island forming Nos.1 and 2 Platforms was added.

Looking south along No.4 Platform: notice the scissors crossings between No.4 Platform line and the No.4 up through line. There were a number of other crossings hereabouts and the Scissors Crossing Cabin, sometimes known as No.3 Cabin (presumably on the assumption that 'A' and 'B' cabins were Nos.1 and 2) can be seen high up to the left.

Left. The Scissors Crossing Cabin looking south, before any of the re-signalling works got underway in this part of the station. No.5 platform to left and No.4 to right.

Below. Crewe South Junction looking north before the re-signalling; old South Junction cabin to left. Imagine a driver approaching this vast array of semaphore signals and having to know which one applied to which lines, especially at night when he would have to count from one side to the other the number of red and green lights and work out which ones applied to his train!

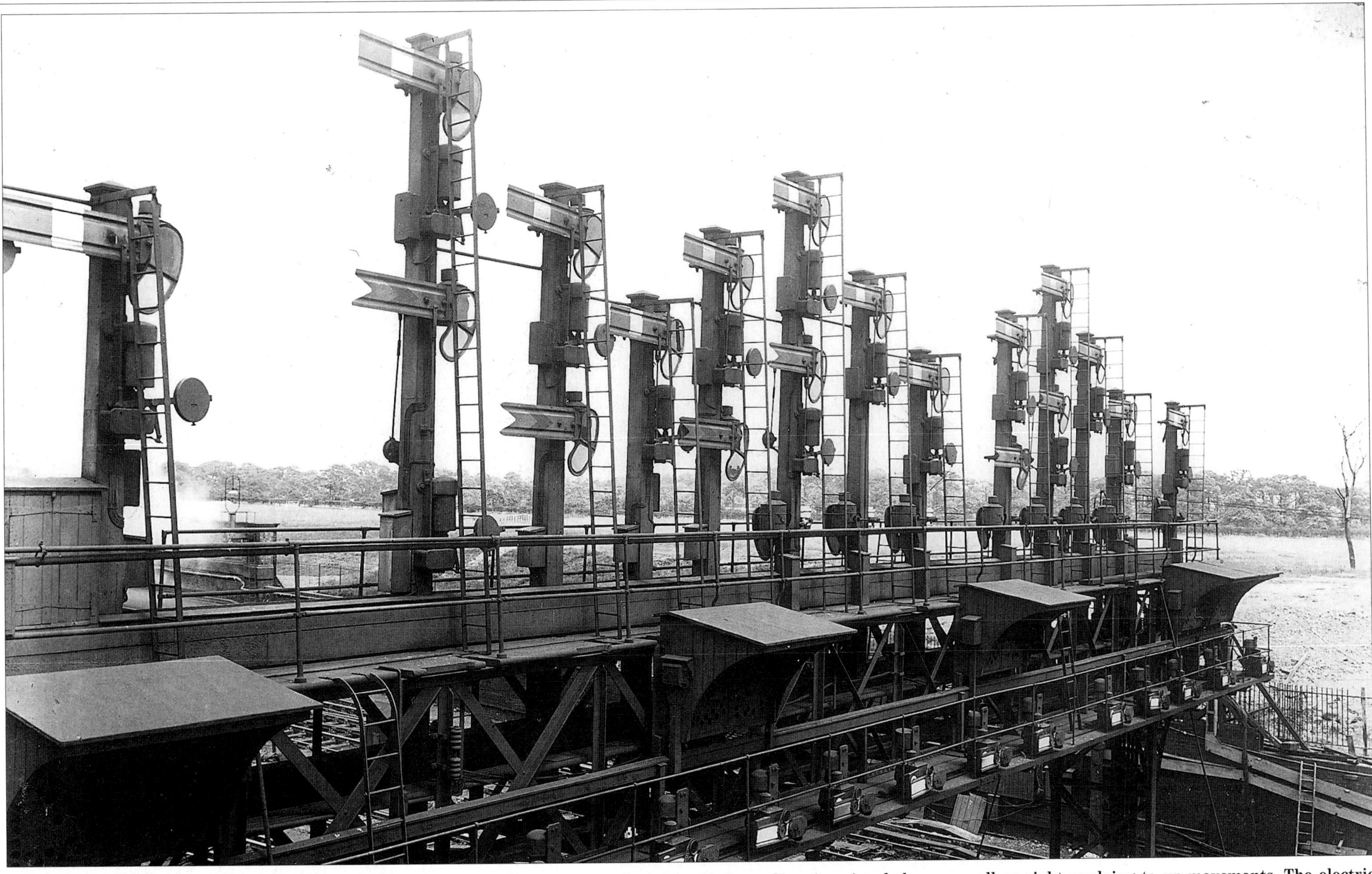

Another view of the South Junction gantry, taken in the 1930s. There were no less than 23 down direction signals here as well as eight applying to up movements. The electric solenoid motors for operating the signal arms on the Webb-Thompson patent can be clearly seen. Notice at the bottom level of the gantry a series of 13 'calling on' arms; there were two more off the picture to the left, and these are not included in the 23 above! They too, were solenoid operated. The box type structures are early forms of route indicator. The Midland Roll Makers factory later occupied the green fields to the right.

The South Junction gantry after re-signalling, a much 'cleaner' layout and thus not nearly as interesting. The vehicles to the left are in the Down Yard, used for the marshalling of non-passenger carrying coaching stock. The signal in the centre is showing a double amber caution aspect for a movement via No.2 Through road.

Crewe South Junction, a view taken from the old signal cabin prior to the re-signalling. The four hip roofed structures of the station can be made out; from left to right they cover No.1 and 2 Platform island, the space between No.1 and 2 Platform island, No.3 and 4 Platform island and No.5 and 6 Platform island. Note that only between the No.1 and 2 and No.2 and 3 islands was the area covered over the through roads, and this was doubtless because this part of the station originated much later than the rest. The high building to centre left is the 'new' station administration block built as a part of the turn of the century remodelling works when the No.1 and 2 Platform island was added. Down Yard to left with the road access to Crewe South shed to the extreme left. The Horse Landing was between this road and the station.

Left and below. **The interior of the old South Junction cabin in 1939, showing the Webb Thompson miniature electric frames. Notice the twin levels of levers and the gap between the frames to give access to clean the windows. The multitude of instruments, signal indicators, rotary route indicators and the like are all well worthy of study. The plate on the end of the frame reads: L&WR Rly Co, Makers Crewe Works FW Webb Patent AM Thompson. Just as drivers had to work out which signals applied to their trains, signalmen had to remember which instruments applied to which routes!**

The new concrete 'bomb proof' South Junction box with its camouflage paint. The large raised wording Crewe South Junction was not added until after the cessation of hostilities, but the fixing arrangements can be seen below the windows.

A view from the south end of No.4 Platform looking south with the re-signalling works underway – note the new gantry behind the old one. Beyond and to the right of the large gantry in the distance, itself the subject of earlier views, is the old South Junction cabin and, to the left, the concrete structure for the new box. Just visible through the gantry is the Carriage Shed.

View from the same point after completion of the re-signalling – once again the ‘cleaning up’ has robbed the scene of much interest. I suspect the bogie vehicle in the centre of the nearest of the two rakes to the left is one of the ex-Midland Railway theatrical scenery vans.

A fine panoramic of the South Junction, from a vantage point in the old cabin. To the left is the former North Staffordshire route to Stoke and Derby, known to Crewe men right up until the 1970s at least, as the ‘Knotty’, with the Carriage Shed to its right. The main line south passes to the right of this shed, and that to Salop to the extreme right. Centre distance is the South shed, and the vehicles in the foreground are in the Down, or as it was sometimes called, Old Yard. In the right distance can just be made out the Goods Tranship Shed, or ‘Warehouse’ as it was sometimes referred to. In the area between the main line south and the South shed was a Permanent Way Department yard where material was stored and track layouts made up and tested prior to installation. The area extreme right was much later occupied by the Diesel Depot yard.

Crewe Basford Hall Junction looking north with the re-signalling works underway; the signal box can be seen just beyond the bridge. This box was retained in the re-signalling works and the Webb tumbler frame and interlocking was modified to operate the electric colour light signals. It was never fitted with the Webb-Thompson arrangement. Therefore, the signals, as can be seen here, were operated by conventional wire and pulley arrangements and the points were operated by rodding. The Independent lines and the routes into Basford Hall Marshalling Yard just can be seen diverging to the left under the bridge. The lines in the foreground are from left to right: down slow; up slow; down fast; up fast.

The new South Junction gantry and signal box, again looking south. The line diverging away to the right is that to Shrewsbury, always known to Crewe men as 'Salop', and just to the right is the Down Yard Pilot, one of the ubiquitous 3F tanks always known to Crewe men incidentally, as 'Humpies'. Note that like its predecessor this gantry carries signals for movements in both directions. In the right distance can be seen the South shed coaling tower.

Good Friday 1960: 1. Royal Scot 46146 THE RIFLE BRIGADE, just north of Hartford Junction twelve miles north of Crewe and passing the exchange sidings with the ICI private railway to Northwich, on Good Friday 15 April 1960. The train is the 8.23am from Workington to Euston, and this Camden based engine would have come on to the train at Preston. (Michael Mensing)

Good Friday 1960: 2. Duchess Pacific 46252 CITY OF LEICESTER approaching Hartford Junction with a relief train from Glasgow to Euston on Good Friday 15 April 1960. This train would have been running behind the 'Royal Scot', which would have left Glasgow Central at 10.00am, and would have been due to leave Crewe at 2.36pm. The time of this photograph is 2.35pm only four minutes after the passing of THE RIFLE BRIGADE. The engine, a Crewe North one, would have come on to the train at Carlisle – note amount of coal in tender – and would be working through to Euston. (Michael Mensing)

Interval 2: Crewe Surroundings

Good Friday 1960: 3. Hartford Junction, but looking in the opposite direction, Good Friday 15 April 1960. Duchess Pacific 46238 CITY OF CARLISLE also has a relief train; note the W reporting number, indicating Euston-Glasgow. This engine was allocated to Carlisle, where indeed it spent much of its life. To the left is a foundation hole for one of the masts for the impending electrification. (Michael Mensing)

Electrification work is well under way south of Alderley Edge on the line from Crewe to Manchester on Good Friday 27 March 1959. The train is the Kingswear portion of the 10.35am Manchester to Cardiff and Kingswear, running as a separate portion on this occasion – the Cardiff portion was in front. The engine is one of the Caprotti Class 5s, 44741 of Longsight shed. (Michael Mensing)

Longsight shed used its Britannia Pacifics on the London jobs from the first, until they were displaced by diesels. Some of these trains were routed via Stoke-on-Trent rather than Crewe, and here is one, the 10.20am from Euston to Manchester, passing Prestbury north-west of Macclesfield on Good Friday 27 March 1959. The engine is 70031 BYRON, and the time 2.53pm. (Michael Mensing)

During the electrification works on the main line north and between Weaver Junction and Crewe, trains were often diverted on Sundays and here is one such working, on Sunday 5 March 1961, near Sandbach on the Manchester line. The train is the Glasgow and Edinburgh to Birmingham, and the time 4.14pm – it would have left Glasgow at 9.25am and was due in Crewe at 3.45pm, so it is running about three quarters of an hour late – note the tender has little coal left in it! 46255 CITY OF HEREFORD was a Carlisle engine and would have come through from Glasgow, to be changed at Crewe. (Michael Mensing)

Shape of things to come, class AM4 (later Class 304) electric multiple unit leaving Sandbach working the 4.3pm from Crewe to Manchester, on Sunday 5 March 1961. Just to the left of the rear vehicle can be seen the then new Sandbach power signal box, and on the right the line curving away to Middlewich and Northwich. (Michael Mensing)

Edge Hill Patriot 45539 E.C. TRENCH, on Good Friday 4 April 1958, climbing the 1 in 177 of Madeley Bank south of Crewe. The train is the 4.45pm Liverpool to Birmingham, passing Chorlton three miles south of Crewe. (Michael Mensing)

Class 5 45448 at Chorlton on Good Friday, 4 April 1958, with the 9.25am Glasgow to Birmingham. The engine, an Aston (Birmingham) one, would in all probability have replaced a Pacific at Crewe. (Michael Mensing)

Rebuilt Patriot 45521 RHYL heads north at Chorlton on Good Friday 1958 with the 12.55pm Euston to Blackpool and Barrow. An Edge Hill engine at the time, it would doubtless work through to Preston. (Michael Mensing)

One more shot at Chorlton on Good Friday 1958, this time showing the 2.10pm Liverpool to Euston, with Jubilee 45554 ONTARIO. This was an Edge Hill engine and would be working through to Euston. The train has around 16 coaches, a tough assignment for a class 6 engine. The 1 in 177 gradient here, whilst not appearing too steep, often made life difficult for crews, especially if the engine was starting 'cold' from Crewe. (Michael Mensing)

Easter Monday 15 April 1963 at Whitchurch, with WR 'Warship' D828 MAGNIFICENT entering the station from Shrewsbury. The train is the 8.0am Plymouth and Kingswear to Liverpool, with through coaches to Manchester and Glasgow. After the electrification of the lines from Crewe to Liverpool and Manchester, rather than take the WR engine off at Shrewsbury and then the Midland Region one in its turn at Crewe, to be replaced it by electric traction, many trains continued through to Crewe with the Western motive power, as was the case here. (Michael Mensing)

A post-war shot of Pacific 46251, still with LMS insignia, on a northbound Scottish train at Lichfield Trent Valley on 26 June 1948. The reporting number would indicate that this is the 1.30pm from Euston to Glasgow, latterly the Mid-Day Scot, due to pass Lichfield at 3.30pm. This was a Carlisle engine at the time although it transferred to Camden in July that year – unfortunately the shed plate cannot be discerned. (FW Shuttleworth)

Chapter Four

The Perth Job

There would be little doubt in your mind, once you had done it, that the hardest regular steam footplate jobs in this country were the nightly 'double home' (for 'double home' read 'lodging') Crewe to Perth turns. Doubtless too, for those devotees of Swindon and Doncaster who have not done it, this statement will bring out the partisan feelings. I reckon that the nearest contenders were the Shrewsbury to Plymouth turns, shared by men from Salop and Laira, with Castle class engines also on 'double home' turns but in this case in daylight hours. However, the Crewe to Perth diagrams were the exclusive preserve of Crewe North men, two jobs each way each night, and part of the North Shed No.2 Link. Perth men, incidentally, never came to Crewe and on the odd occasions when Crewe men did not work right through, Christmas Eve for example, the crews changed over at Carlisle.

The No.2 link consisted of eight sets of men in an eight week roster, each set completing three 'double home' trips to Perth during two of the eight weeks, and two return trips during a further five weeks. During the remaining week they worked 'double home' trips to Glasgow, out and home with the Mid Day Scot, largely to retain route knowledge and of course, in the winter the only time they saw daylight from the footplate! Operation of these trains by Crewe men goes back to the early 1930s; indeed not long after the 'Royal Scot' class engines were introduced, with which the practice of through working of engines and men commenced. The trains concerned were the nightly London to Aberdeen and Inverness jobs, with through coaches to places like Oban, Fort William and as far north as Lairg. The Lairg coaches, so far as I am aware, formed the longest regular advertised through coach journey that could be made in this country, a situation that existed for many years. North shed men worked these trains – they left Euston around 8 o' clock each evening – between Crewe and Perth, lodging at Perth and returning the following night. For great parts of the journey, and in particular over the banks north of Preston and Carlisle, they were heavily loaded – often to 16 vehicles – which included the heavy six wheel sleeping cars.

Naturally, the trains commanded Pacifics from these engines' inception, originally the Princess Royals, known to Crewe men as 'Lizzies' and, almost as soon as they were introduced, the subsequent 'Coronation' class, the 'Big 'Uns'. These engines were indeed magnificent machines and you only have to see one in the flesh, never mind ride on one, to appreciate the Crewe men's sobriquet. Again I fear, my own partisanship will be brought into question but to my mind, appreciative as I am of the efforts of Swindon and Doncaster, these 'High Born Ladies' of the Iron Road were the finest express passenger locomotives ever to grace the railways in this country. And what more splendid names could be found for such beasts?

As a brief aside, it was the night diagrams which meant that not all were painted red in BR days. As the adoption of this colour scheme entailed additional costs some 'boffin' decided that there was little point incurring such expense on engines that were hardly ever seen in daylight! Hence, before the diesels started to arrive and disrupt things, those allocated to sheds with a predominance of night diagrams remained in green and this of course, included the Crewe North complement. The Polmadie engines remained green too, the authorities north of the border

Duchess Pacific 46244 KING GEORGE V1, outside the shed at Perth on 16 May 1964. Unfortunately not a Crewe North engine, rather one allocated at the time to Carlisle Kingmoor, and a picture taken long after Crewe North had stopped sending its Pacifics so far north on any regular basis. However, it does show a 'Big 'Un' at Perth. Notice the jib of the breakdown crane, and what looks like a V2 in the background. (Frank Hornby)

A view from the steps of the footbridge which went from the north end of No.1 platform to the North shed, and Pacific 46230 DUCHESS OF BUCCLEUCH. Having left the North shed, it is now backing down to clear the points (seen underneath) before going forward to await its train from the south, which it will take forward. It was a Polmadie engine for most of its life, from 1941 until withdrawal; unfortunately this view is undated, but around 1958 I would say as she still carries the earlier BR emblem on the tender. The steam from the rear of the tender is from the coal pusher engine exhaust indicating the valves blowing through slightly. (JB Bucknall)

never wanting to have anything to do with the LMS in the first place! The men had a great affection for these locomotives, if for no other reason that if looked after correctly and fired to their liking, they could always be relied on the beat the efforts of any fireman. Good enginemen will warm to any engine whose prowess is directly related to their efforts, and whose upper limits it was almost impossible to achieve. Despite both fireman and driver getting wet shirts, a 'Big 'Un' always appeared to be capable of just that little bit more.

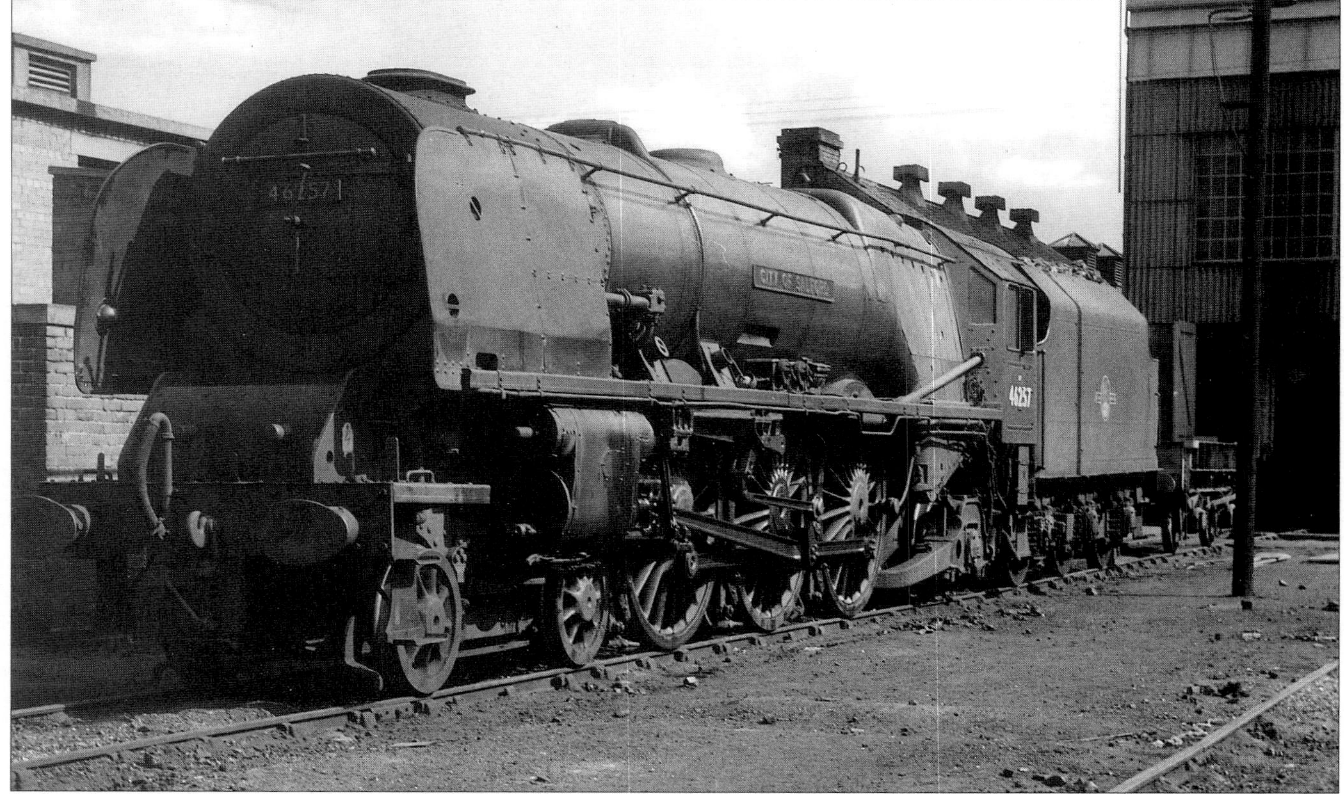

A Kingmoor 'Big 'Un' outside the Repair Shed at Perth. The very last one built, 46257 CITY OF SALFORD has the modified rear end including the Delta trailing truck. Perth had quite a large Repair Shop which came under the control of St Rollox Works, and not the local Motive Power people. One wonders what it was doing there being a Carlisle engine, as Carlisle also had an 'Outstation Repair Shop', as they were called. The picture is unfortunately undated, but I would place it at about 1960; certainly not much earlier as the engine already has the electrification warning notices fitted, and they date from that year.

One of the late George Wheeler's fine portraits. Carlisle's 46234 DUCHESS OF ABERCORN is at the south end of Crewe station, having perhaps worked a train from the north, in which case it will be running back light to the North shed. The picture is undated but 46234 was transferred to Carlisle in November 1959 after a long period at Crewe North. The overhead wires are already in position so I'd guess the period as the summer of 1960. In view of the headlight code and the new-looking paint around the smokebox, however, she could be waiting to work a running-in turn on the Shrewsbury line after attention in the Works. (Late George Wheeler)

No self-respecting North shed man could hold his head up high unless he had been to Perth on a 'Big 'Un', so to Perth on a 'Big 'Un' I made it my business to go! The men in the No.2 link were a breed on their own, and this link never really featured in the routine progression of men on seniority through the links at Crewe: the men either loved or hated it, with every job a 'double home' one. As a consequence the men either jumped the normal progression when a vacancy appeared, or remained in lower links until their turn came to jump over the No.2 link and go straight into the No.1 link – which despite long distance jobs had less lodging turns and more daylight! But then, the No.2 paid very well! Imagine then these hardy souls setting off for Perth up to three times in any seven days, returning on three more, with anything up to 600 tons behind the tender for parts of the trip and with the prospect of 296 miles to go! And there were the banks of Grayrigg, Shap, Beattock and Kinbuck, and the best part of ten tons of coal to shift in around six hours. These then were the Perth jobs, and yes, I had to go to Perth!

So it came about that having got to know Driver George Preece well, when he had a period on 'shed duties' following an illness, that I joined him and his mate one night for an unrepeatable experience. I only went to Perth once on a steam engine and as by this time the diesels had already started to infiltrate the workings, George arranged with the Running Foreman to be sure we had a 'Big 'Un' on the Friday night chosen – they did retain some of the Perth diagrams until well into the diesel era, but you had to make sure... After finishing work that Friday I went round to George's house (he lived near the shed right by the *Brunswick Hotel* in Nantwich Road) and his good wife fed and watered me before we set off back to the shed. On the way, of course, it was necessary to join other crews partaking of traditional liquid refreshment at the *Queens Hotel* right outside the shed entrance in Station Street – see Chapter One for more of this noble establishment. All 'good' locomotive sheds had a watering hole close by!

We were booked to take over the 11.17pm to Inverness as far as Perth, leaving Euston at 7.15; we were due off the shed at about ten minutes to eleven, and I have the relevant timetables by me as I write. Now, despite the engines being prepared for the Perth Link by a preparation crew, the regular men considered it their preserve, and theirs alone, to make the final inspection and adjustments and nobody denied them this. So, suitably refreshed, at about 10 o' clock we made our way into the shed ensuring I was unseen (though many of my 'mates' knew what I was up to!) by both the Running Foreman and the Leading Fitter as George and his Mate booked on.

At the engine arrangements board I noted our engine was 46235 CITY OF BIRMINGHAM, a long-time Crewe North resident, stabled on No.25 road in that part of the yard known as 'The Coal Hole'. For George and his mate this was a three-trip week, so they had been backwards and forwards to Perth twice already and with this same engine on the second trip; hence George had asked for it again on this occasion. It would in all probability have either stood all day on the shed, or perhaps made a return trip to Shrewsbury on one of the West of England jobs which was often the case with these engines between trips north of the border. In earlier times it had been the practice to keep the same engines on the jobs for weeks on end, unless they were stopped for 'X' examinations or whatever.

So the three of us made our way to No.25 road and as George attended to the inner needs of the engine with an oil can, Frank the fireman – I cannot for the life of me recall his surname, although I can see him now – went about the Crewe practice of 'filling the box'. This consisted of opening the tender coal chute doors and as the tender was full, this entailed use of the coal pick to force up the retaining arms. In addition the job required not a little dexterity from whoever performed it, as it was accompanied by around two tons of coal finding its way onto the footplate. If you weren't careful, you could be almost buried under the avalanche! Then,

Lancaster on 20 June 1963, with 46256 SIR WILLIAM A STANIER FRS stopped to detach a vehicle from a northbound van train. By this time these engines were eking out their time on such lesser duties. (FW Shuttleworth)

aided and abetted by one of the shed steam raisers, the whole lot was shovelled onto the fire without, it appeared to me, any particular method in mind. The shovelling continued until it was possible to close the tender doors again. Any lumps too big to go on the shovel were man-handled in, and any too big to go through the fire hole were broken up with the pick. At the conclusion of this exercise, to my inexperienced eyes at least, the fire appeared to be completely out and the heap of coal almost touching the brick arch!

After this and following George's return, the footplate was hosed down and we crept back under the coaling plant to top up the tender. Now Crewe North got ample supplies of good North Staffordshire hards, including the famous Woodhead seam from Foxfield Colliery near Cheadle, as well as limited supplies of Welsh steam coal. When it was available, the latter was always kept for the Scottish jobs, the coal hole attendants ensuring its delivery into the hopper at the right time. Timing was vital, for our colleagues on the 10.13 ex-Crewe, The Royal Highlander, also with a 'Big 'Un' on this occasion, would have been right in front of us under the hopper with a similar top-up in mind, and the No.1 Link Glasgow men would be in our wake. There was of course, method in this apparent madness because Perth only got supplies of soft Scottish coal, with not nearly as many BTUs as that to be had further south. With such a large fire – despite looking as if it had gone out, it seemed – and a tender heaped well beyond its nominal capacity, only the minimum amount of coal would be taken on at Perth so that when the climbing started in earnest on the return journey (they always came back with the same engine) on leaving Carlisle, the shovel might again bite into the North Staffordshire 'hards' or Welsh steam coal!

We 'rang off' the shed just about right time and ran back onto No.2 Through Road at the station to attach two bogie mail vans. These were to be added to the train when it arrived and before running forward onto the Down Liverpool Slow, to await the train. Being allowed to occupy this position was a clear indication that our train was on time, so that we would be ready to propel back just a soon as the inward engine was detached. It arrived behind a Type 4 diesel and we were soon coupling 46235 on, a task performed by the Station Shunter rather than Frank, as it was a coach attachment rather than the engine. Frank had already coupled us to the two coaches; these demarcation rules were strictly adhered to in those days. The Guard came forward to tell us we had 14 on and he would have also told us the weight, which I cannot now remember, but it would have been around 540 tons. We got the right way on time as I recall, though I did manage to make a few notes on the trip and I still have the grubby notebook I used to carry round, mainly to record the numbers of the engines I worked on. The jet had been hard on since we left the shed and believe it or not I could see a glimmer of flame from the fire, the steam pressure having risen from about the 150lb which was all we had when we got on the engine, to about 200lb. This seemed to me rather low to start a journey of this magnitude; the working pressure of the boiler on these engines was 250lb but it did not seem to bother either George or Frank.

Although we had a heavy train the timings were quite tight between stops and as I said earlier I have the relevant timetables by me as I write. The Perth trains always tended to make quite a lot of stops, for all sorts of reasons, not least attaching and detaching vehicles, loading and unloading mail and the like. Indeed, we were booked to stop at Wigan, Preston, Carlisle, Carstairs, Motherwell, Mossend Yard – to detach some of the postal vehicles – Larbert, Stirling, Gleneagles and of course Perth. The through Oban coaches were detached at Stirling. Between Crewe and Preston I see we were allowed no less than 80 minutes for the 61 miles. With not much more than 30% cut-off and three quarters regulator, except for the sharp rise on leaving Wigan (I in 104) to Boar's Head, we ambled along at not much more than 60 mph with steam pressure holding its own at about the same 200lb as when we left Crewe. It all seemed too easy to me, and somewhat unexciting. But it was a bright clear night in early September, on the eve of the winter timetable and George told me the loadings were still quite heavy. The engine made a good clean start from Wigan and sounded well pounding up past Ryland's Siding and I did note that the exhaust injector had been set on leaving Crewe. Apart from when we were stopped at Wigan it had been on almost continuously, changing over between exhaust and live steam beautifully as and when the regulator was opened and closed. Even in my limited experience of steam locomotive maintenance at the time, we always seemed to be doing some sort of work on these items of equipment!

All of this time the fire had not been touched and it was not until we approached Preston and were passing Farrington Curve Junction that the dampers were fully opened as the fire really began to burn through. I remember realising that it had been judicious use of the dampers that had kept the steam pressure constant so far, but once fully opened at this point they were not touched again until we arrived at Perth. At Preston we acquired two more coaches, the Liverpool and Manchester sleepers, and the Guard came forward to tell us of this; the Guards on these jobs by the way were also Crewe men and they too, worked the same diagrams as the footplate men. As we stood in the station the steam pressure gradually rose, such that the safety valves were sizzling as departure time approached. We seemed to be at Preston an age, and I see the timetable shows a ten-minute station time.

We got away from Preston on time I think, or as near to as not to matter (I was of course no O.S. Nock or C.J. Allen, although I had been an avid reader of their articles and books from just about as soon as I could read) and then the real action started – we might have been on a Sunday School Excursion hitherto! Once clear of the station and on the sharp rise to Oxheys Frank started to shovel, and shovel with vigour, the fire by this time being well burnt through. He fired continuously except when pausing to operate the water scoop on Brock thoughts, until George closed the regulator for the decent into Lancaster. This was despite the fact that this twenty mile section was almost flat. We rolled through the gentle curve at Lancaster station and on over the River Lune bridge on this extremely clear and moonlit night, and then onwards to the almost flat seven mile section skirting Morecambe Bay onwards to Carnforth. No more coal was added to the fire on this stretch, and again 30% cut-off or thereabouts and three quarters regulator was enough to keep us bowling along in the 65-70 mph range. I noticed that Frank's firing was extremely systematic, spreading the coal around the box and with great dexterity keeping the back corners filled by a twist with the shovel as it entered the box. I was to learn later that the knack of making these engines steam well was to keep those back corners full, and it often took men some time to master this – remember the grate area of these engines was no less than 50 square feet and the far corners were a long way from the door!

I had for most of the time so far positioned myself behind George, actually standing on the tender just behind the fall plate, but during the prolonged period of firing as we left Preston I used the Fireman's seat. During this time I frequently looked back, especially on curves, and what a magnificent sight it was to behold. This enormous train had lights only on parts of it, as the sleeping cars dotted throughout were almost completely darkened. Gracefully it followed the stream of smoke from the engine, highlighted by the moonlight. And to listen to that distinctive and characteristic 'thumping' of a Duchess four-cylinder exhaust, was quite something. I can tell you now that to ride on one of these truly magnificent machines and on a still clear moonlit night, with approaching 600 tons behind the tender and at speeds in the 70s, was the thrill of a lifetime. I only did it once, but that memory of CITY OF BIRMINGHAM riding like the wonderful lady she was, without a perceptible mechanical knock anywhere, a vehicle completely in sympathy with its task and accomplished with apparent and commensurate ease, will stay with me until the end of my days. Oh, how I wish I had done it more often, for although I had several subsequent trips on these engines, apart from the trip back from Perth the following Saturday night, I never again rode one in the hours of darkness.

As a short diversion from our story, I later came to know the north road extremely well, especially as far as Carlisle, but also to a lesser extent by both the Caledonian and Glasgow & South Western routes, onwards to Glasgow. I travelled these routes on numerous occasions, usually associated with problems on the Brush Type 4s as we called them then (later Class 47s) or the D400s (later Class 50s). So much so that I felt I would have been able to 'sign' the routes if I had had to! The ex-LNWR route to Carlisle and the Caledonian route to Glasgow are wonderful railways and I still try to travel them occasionally these days. However, I only went to Perth again on the footplate from Crewe twice, once on an EE Type 4 (later Class 40) and once on a D400; it was shortly after this last trip that Crewe men's workings through to Perth ceased, with the countrywide reduction in lodging turns. I did, however, join the men on their footplates and travel the section between Greenhill Junction and Perth many times after I took charge at Eastfield some twenty years later.

Firing commenced again at Carnforth and apart from a short relapse passing Burton & Holme, and again when we took water on Dillicar troughs, continued almost without a break until we were within a few hundred yards of Shap Summit – some 25 miles I hasten to add. As we approached Milnthorpe where the climbing really starts we were doing almost 80 mph and George pushed the regulator hard over onto the second valve, and big guy as he was this took some effort, it was the first time he had done so since we left Crewe – but the cut-off remained at around 30%. Now 46235 started to talk to the sky, and although the beat began to slow down, gradually at first, the noise was much greater.

From Milnthorpe to the foot of Grayrigg Bank at Oxenholme the average gradient over the almost seven miles is 1 in 160, steepening at the latter place to around three miles each of 1 in 131 and 1 in 104 – this is Grayrigg itself. Now many enginemen consider the long slog from Milnthorpe to Grayrigg, 13 miles or so, to be a harder part of the climb over the fells than Shap itself, and bank engines were available at both Oxenholme and Tebay, or a pilot could be taken from Oxenholme right through to Shap Summit. However, there was almost an unwritten law among Crewe men not to take bank engines or pilots, unless things were really bad – tonight was to be no exception. As the engine tackled the ever-increasing grades, with Frank on the shovel continuously, George gradually lengthened the cut-off as the speed dropped. I would make no judgement myself on the merits or otherwise of the six miles of Grayrigg, versus the four at 1 in 75 of Shap, in so far as to which was the toughest. But to be with 46235 that night was awe-inspiring, the like of which I have never experienced since, and I have travelled on steam locomotive footplates in many parts of the world.

Speed dropped rapidly it seemed, as did the water in the glass and we were down to about 50 mph at Oxenholme with the cut-off at about 50%. Yet this great lady held the speed at between 30 and 35 mph and when Frank paused for a moment to put on the live steam injector to supplement the exhaust one, the boiler pressure started to drop. What a spectacle and what a sound, as we pounded our way, pounded being the operative word, the lonely signalmen in Lambrigg and Mosedale Crossing boxes silhouetted against the box oil lamps making a memorable sight. It was here incidentally, that I remember realising that we had not seen an adverse signal since leaving Preston and I marvelled how George could spot those oil-lit semaphore distants which were

A beautiful view in the Lune Gorge, Saturday 18 August 1962. Crewe North 'Big 'Un' 46235 CITY OF BIRMINGHAM is on the Saturday-only 10.27am Glasgow to Euston, which it would work as far as Crewe. The train is rounding the curve at Low Gill and the branch to Ingleton can just be seen curving away above the train. The rake of coaches consists of the 'Caledonian' set, augmented and not otherwise used at a weekend. The engine is in lovely condition, a-long term Crewe North resident and the one I travelled on when I went to Perth. And, would you believe it, Driver George Preece is at the regulator! A magnificent backcloth to a magnificent engine, where better can Stanier's masterpieces be seen than in these surroundings? (GW Morrison)

46235

Dillicar water troughs, south of Tebay, with 46236 CITY OF BRADFORD getting a good fill before tackling Shap, on 25 April 1962. Once again the magnificent backcloth of the Lune Gorge is there to be savoured. (FW Shuttleworth)

frequently so high up. I realised later that the men depended on getting a clear run from Carnforth; if they did not it almost certainly meant they would have to take assistance with a load the like of which we had behind the tender on this night!

With Grayrigg taken in our stride boiler pressure was down to about 220lb and despite both injectors being on the water was only showing half a glass. As speed began to rise on the seven mile level and downhill section on towards Tebay, I observed that George, despite shortening the cut-off, left the regulator hard over until speed approached 70 when he brought it right back onto the small valve, completely closing it at one point. Except when he stopped to operate the water scoop and get a full tank on Dillicar troughs, Frank had fired almost continuously from below Oxenholme. Since those early days I have come to love this part of the country and I consider the line from around Milnthorpe to Shap as my favourite, in this country at least. And on this still moonlight night the magnificent Lune Gorge took on a special significance for me, here like nowhere else I feel, do the hills, fells, valley, river and railway come together in such perfect sympathy, and in such a complementary way. And on a moonlit late summer night it can be seen to its best, the glow from our fire and the spray from the water as we filled the tank on the troughs accentuating the scene; on this occasion one that remains as clear to me now as it did then.

With water duly taken Frank and George changed places as we approached Tebay and the four miles plus of 1 in 75. With an almost full glass of water and the safety valves simmering the live steam injector was shut off and the first thing Frank did on getting into the Driver's seat was to heave the regulator onto its stop again and let the wheel down to 40% or thereabouts. As the speed dropped he continued to lengthen the cut-off and once again we heard that sheer cacophony of noise, but the speed was dropping rapidly and the cut-off was dropping too, 45, 50, 55 and at Scout Green, with speed about 25 mph, 60% – almost but not quite, all she had got.

All this time George was firing with the exhaust shooting sky high and the glow from the fire hole door lighting up the countryside adjacent to the cab door openings; they were truly sights and sensations never to be forgotten. Unlike Grayrigg which is largely in a cutting, Shap is wild and exposed, and in such surroundings 46235 seemed to me like a wild animal truly at home for she was talking to all who would listen, and oh, what a voice she had. It was soon after Scout Green that George, perspiring heavily, gave up the struggle and handed the shovel back to Frank. We were almost at the Summit by this time and George had to wait for his eyes to become accustomed to the dark again; before leaving the Driver's seat Frank put the live steam injector on, as the water was well down in the glass – between here and the Summit I noticed that the steam pressure dropped to just above the 200lb mark. How I wished I could have helped them with the firing, but such experience as I had had by this stage in my career was very limited and I would not have been equal to the task!

The firing effort so far sufficed to take us over the Summit, the engine holding her feet perfectly, but I was left wondering how they managed when the climatic conditions were not so favourable. They assured me that with a clear road in any weather conditions the banks were tackled unaided. Like Grayrigg, once over the Summit the regulator was left hard over and the cut-off rapidly shortened until speed reached around 75 mph, when it was eased right back. There was now a period of comparative tranquillity after the previous hour or so as we sped down the long grades towards Penrith, and on towards Carlisle. The live steam injector remained on until we had a full glass of water and apart from a few

The up Royal Scot leaving Carlisle on 18 September 1956, with Pacific 46229 DUCHESS OF HAMILTON, a Camden engine at the time and working home. It would have come on to the train at Carlisle. A lovely atmospheric view. (FW Shuttleworth)

The down Royal Scot with no less than seventeen vehicles in tow on a Sunday (obviously a busy one) 14 August 1960. The engine is Polmadie's 46232 DUCHESS OF MONTROSE; surprising dirty for the time, she would have come on the train at Carlisle and is seen here passing Kingmoor, about to cross over onto the up line as single line working was in operation. With a load of this size the train would undoubtedly have taken banking assistance over Beattock. Notice the freight in the loop waiting to follow with Class 5 45473 in charge. (GW Morrison)

short rounds on the fire, steam pressure rallying round, we motored along at speeds approaching 80 mph apart from the 60 mph restriction round the curves at Penrith. Tea was brewed on this section and we had a sandwich – George's wife had included me in George's rations that night! The ride of the engine was most impressive as she rolled round the curving section north of Penrith, it seemed to me almost as good as a coach.

We were booked to stop at the Border City for about 15 minutes and we came to a perfect stop, at about 2.30am I think, George making a text book stop right against the water column. Carlisle, I recall, was busy that night with mail trains and the like and several light engine movements. Frank was down in a jiff and the 'bag' was in the tank and I was trusted to the only job I did all night, operating the water valve to Frank's instructions, while George took a look around our engine with his oil feeder. What stood out in my mind at this stage of the journey was how tightly timed we were. Despite being allowed around two hours from Preston we had only just about kept time and I did not see how we could have done it any quicker. The engine, it seemed, had been pushed pretty hard since passing Carnforth and had given about all it could on the banks, especially Shap. By any standards we had not been hanging about! And if we had had to stop to take a banker or pilot we must have lost time and would have been late at Carlisle.

At the expense of repeating myself, perhaps my overriding impression, not least as I reflect on the experience 40 years later, was how sure-footed the locomotive was. George told me afterwards, as indeed did other drivers, that provided the steam sanding equipment was working correctly even in the autumnal mists and fogs they would manage without assistance, and they gave special attention to the sand gear on preparation of the engines at both Crewe and Perth – and of course, the loads were much lighter outside of the Summer timetable. With good sanding, George reckoned a 'Big 'Un' would always hold its feet and in his 20-odd years in the Perth Link as fireman and driver, he had never stalled on any of the banks despite on occasions being stopped for signals.

There was time at Carlisle for another cup of tea, a chat with the guard and a few rounds on the fire before departure, with some 90 minutes for the section over Beattock to our next stop at Carstairs. We got away on time I think, or as near to it as not to matter, but we still had the full trailing load on the next 74 mile section. And there was the ten miles of almost 1 in 75 of Beattock bank yet to come. But it was a reasonably easy run along the flat five or six miles to Gretna, followed by an undulating 35 miles or so to the foot of the bank. The plain country of the Solway Firth and the large tracts of open countryside make quite a contrast to the more wooded and enclosed run down from Shap. Half to three quarter's regulator and 20-30% cut-off kept us bowling along in the 70s with the exhaust almost inaudible.

The fire was well burnt through on leaving Carlisle, and the occasional round kept the boiler pressure in the 235–240 range, the exhaust injector again keeping the water in the top quarter of the glass. Opportunity was taken on this stretch to operate the coal pusher on the tender, and after a number of operations of this very useful bit of kit several tons of coal became far more easily accessible than hitherto. I reflected that it would be much more of a task to work these trains with a 'Lizzie', without the luxury of this equipment. Once over the small summit at Wamphray, Frank started to fire in earnest, and from there until within sight of Beattock Summit firing was almost continuous. By the time George started to open the engine out again the box was getting pretty full.

Like the earlier banks we were going it alone on Beattock and as soon as the 1 in 88 at the foot came in sight (it is that steep you can see the change of levels from the footplate!) the regulator went hard over and the cut-off was dropped down to 45% or thereabouts – but we were going much faster than when we approached either Grayrigg or Shap, about 80 mph I noted. However, the procedure hereafter was much the same, the cut-off being gradually lengthened as speed dropped and we balanced out at some 25 mph and 55-60% cut-off quite soon. Once again our great locomotive was baying at the sky, and just as defiantly as earlier. To some extent it was more impressive this time in the part cuttings and embankments, with dawn breaking on this still, clear night. It's a long climb, and with the water dropping George put the live steam injector on as Frank continued to fire and we were only about half way up! Steam pressure took a real pounding now, being just below 200lb when we eventually got over the top. I took the Fireman's seat during the whole climb as I had earlier, and it was wonderful to lean out and enjoy the still morning, the syncopated exhaust beat and to look back at the long train snaking along behind.

The engine really settled into her stride and it seemed as if she could have just gone on like this forever! But it was a super noise she was making – I can hear her now – a lovely tight front end and as sure footed as if she had been on rubber tyres! The more I write of this trip the more I feel how inadequate my description is of this my most memorable footplate experience, and so early in my career – I was only 16. I recall thinking as I leaned out that night that these engines must be the most impressive man has ever put on rails, and I have to add that nothing I have seen in the intervening forty-odd years has suggested to me that that analysis was in any way wrong! But what a thrashing the engine was taking, small wonder I thought why we had them for a valve and piston exam every 30-36,000 miles, and that they went to works for a repair after about 90,000 miles.

One look at my new-found friends was enough to realise that she could not go on forever. Frank was visibly slowing, pressure was dropping and despite the efforts of both injectors the water level was, very slightly but none the less, dropping. We crept over the top at about 20 mph and as soon as the beat quickened firing stopped and this time the regulator was eased and the cut-off pulled up to about 30%. The engine nevertheless accelerated her enormous train such that in the two miles of 1 in 99 down to Elvanfoot we were up in the 60s. It took quite a time for the water to get back up towards the top nut and for the boiler pressure to rally round. A few rounds on the fire, George having handed over the driving to Frank once more, kept the engine happy and as we had a lengthy stay at Carstairs we did not take water on Strawfrank troughs, but stopped under the water column at Carstairs pretty well on time. It seemed an age detaching the Edinburgh coaches, perhaps because they were not all at the end of the train and required a shunt, such that we were I think, about five or ten minutes late leaving and two coaches lighter. During the stopover George had given the fire quite a lot of attention whilst Frank and I filled the tender, as well as breaking up some large lumps of coal that had appeared on the shovelling plate. With George at the regulator again it then took us some twenty minutes for the fourteen mile sprint to Motherwell where, after a small bout of firing on the short rise to Craigenhill, we made a brief stop. After Motherwell we left the main line at Lesmaghagow Junction and went into Mossend Yard where a service stop was made to detach a further two coaches, leaving twelve for the next stage of the journey.

The real work was now over and an easy job was made of the twenty or so miles to our next stop at Larbert, mostly either on the level through Cumbernauld or down the grades to the plain of the Firth of Forth. Nor was much work needed on towards Stirling where the Oban coaches were detached, leaving nine to go forward to Perth. By this time we were running to time again and of course it was getting quite light – indeed as we stood at Stirling to sun began to appear over the Ochills on what promised to be a super late summer day. Frank, back firing now, put plenty on the fire here, for we had to climb the six miles of 1 in 88 and 1 in 100 of Kinbuck bank. He shovelled away for part of the way up but to all intents and purposes the firing was over. With the reduced load the engine made very light work of the job and although George used full regulator on the bank the cut-off was never much longer than 45%. From Kinbuck to Perth is a lovely stretch of railway and quite a fast one, largely following the course of the River Allan. There are wonderful views of the Ochill Hills on the up side and distant views of the Trosachs and Ben Lomond on the down, the Grampians providing a backcloth to the north.

I got to know this wonderful part of Scotland extremely well during my period at Eastfield as we lived in a small village called Barco, a few miles north of Dunblane on the road to Crieff – very close the Greenloaning. It is indeed a very nice place to live, with some terrific scenery and wildlife. Onwards then we sped on this lovely morning and with a brief stop at Gleneagles to let the golfers off, 46235 bowled along in the upper 70s using but a breath of steam and 15-20% cut-off. There is a sharp down grade at 1 in 100 for a few miles from Gleneagles where speed was allowed to reach 80 and then on through Dunning and Forteviot towards Hilton Junction and Perth. The fire was well burnt through by this time and the disposal crew at Perth were not going to have too much to deal with – I reckoned there was about three tons left in the tender but we must have had at least eleven tons when we left Crewe, and of course about two tons on the fire itself!

We arrived at Perth on time, give or take a few minutes, 296 miles and six hours later, and just about the most memorable six hours in my life, both before and since. We were relieved on arrival by a set of Perth men booked to hook off and take the engine to the shed. I could see two Black Fives ready to take the train on over the Highlands to Inverness – how I wished I could have gone with them, if I could have stayed awake that is! In the event I had to wait until diesel days before I was able to footplate the Highland main line after I was based in Scotland, and that of course was on the diesels. So we made our weary way to the 'Lodge', a super family of a Perth railwayman and oh, what an incredible Scottish breakfast we were treated to, including the proverbial Haggis! And then sleep; the next thing I remember was Frank waking me up: 'come on' he said, 'we have another 296 miles to get home'! Although we were 'booked' to relieve the preparation crew at the station we actually went to the shed to have that final look over the engine. This time the firebox was not filled up with coal as it was before our departure from Crewe. Only the minimum of the local soft Scottish coal was put on the tender so that the shovel would find that good old Staffordshire hards well before we reached home.

We left that evening, 9 o'clock to Euston, another 296 miles as Frank said and this time with the load getting heavier as we went south rather than the other way round, and with another tender full of coal to shift. But then, that is another story!

On Beattock bank itself, Camden Pacific 46242 CITY OF GLASGOW tackles the bank at Greskine with a down Birmingham to Glasgow train on 19 July 1959. With around 16 coaches in tow, notice the exhaust from the banker in the distance. A Camden engine at the time, she would be working through from Crewe to Glasgow, as a part of the two or three day cyclic diagrams in operation at the time to improve the utilisation of these engines. (GW Morrison)

The up Royal Scot passing Harrison Siding, south of Carlisle on the climb to Shap, on Saturday 29 August 1959. The engine is 46243 CITY OF LANCASTER, allocated to Crewe North at the time and probably working through to Euston, again on one of the cyclic diagrams – the gradient here is 1 in 125. (GW Morrison)

Glasgow Central on 21 July 1959 with 46252 CITY OF LANCASTER ready to work the 10.10am to Birmingham. A Crewe North engine, she would work through to Crewe with men from the North shed No.1 link. (GW Morrison)

This picture is to my mind just about the finest portrait ever taken of one of these magnificent locomotives, and it is my all-time favourite. Crewe North's 46241 CITY OF EDINBURGH is leaving Perth in wonderful light on a summer evening in July 1960, with the 8.50pm to Euston past Hilton Junction. North shed men on their way home with 296 miles and ten tons of coal to go. Notice the coal piled high on the tender, the whiff of steam at the safety valves, tight front end with not the slightest steam leak, and the sleeping cars towards the end of the train. This is what these engines were all about, and although this picture has appeared many times before, I make no apology for its inclusion here! (WJV Anderson – courtesy Rail Archive Stephenson)

A stirring action shot of 46227 DUCHESS OF DEVONSHIRE, a Polmadie engine from 1948 until withdrawal in December 1962. In fine fettle, she is ascending Beattock bank at Harthope with a down train, on 4 October 1956. Notice the tight front end and how effective the smoke deflectors are in helping to lift the exhaust clear of the crew's vision. What a lovely picture, showing one of these magnificent machines at their very best, and doing what they were made for. In your author's humble opinion they have no equal in the long annals of locomotive history! But then as one brought up in the territory they worked, and a former Crewe North apprentice, what else could be the case!